*You Can Do This* is so refreshing. With inspiring and funny stories, Tricia helps you exchange fear for faith. She leads you to a place where you can deal with the bullies who have tried to steal your confidence—the ones around you and the ones inside you. Read this book and live as the confident girl and mighty warrior who God intended you to be.

**JENNIFER DUKES LEE**
Author of *The Happiness Dare* and *Love Idol*

They say life doesn't come with an instruction manual, but I think "they"—the authors of such platitudes—have yet to read *You Can Do This*. The wise, quirky voice of Tricia Lott Williford is the one I want to hear. I want to hear it when I don't feel as though I'm good enough. I want to hear it when I feel afraid of what the future might hold. I want her voice in my ear when I meet someone who's unkind. As you read *You Can Do This*, listen for the gentle voice of God's life-giving Spirit breathing through the words on each page.

**MARGOT STARBUCK**
Author of *Small Things with Great Love*

With gentle humor and friendly warmth, Tricia Lott Williford assures women that they can be who God has created them to be. Williford comes alongside the reader as a fellow struggler, not an expert, winsomely and honestly reflecting on mistakes made and lessons learned. I love that Williford incorporates practical examples and advice—both from her life and from other women's—about walking in courage and in God-confidence. Readers who feel alone and insecure (and who hasn't felt that way?) will find much to love in *You Can Do This*, including rest stops (questions and tasks related to biblical confidence) at the end of each chapter.

**DENA DYER**
Coauthor of *Love at First Fight*

Tricia's poignant, humorous writing has always captivated me, but she really hit a home run with *You Can Do This*. The wisdom she imparts on female confidence is fresh and bold and grounded in truth. You'll never look at yourself quite the same. Buy this book for your daughters, your best friends, and most of all, for yourself.

**RACHEL RANDOLPH**
Coauthor of *Nourished: A Search for Health, Happiness, and a Full Night's Sleep*

Even women who stand on platforms can struggle with confidence, and raising small people demands outright guts. Tricia Lott Williford shares hard-won insights and do-it-today ideas to grow stronger. Tricia helps women from all walks of life sit tall in their places at the table—with God and those they're called to love and lead. I loved this book!

**NAOMI CRAMER OVERTON**
Former president/CEO of MOPS International and national director for World Vision's National Leadership Council

# you can do This

## Seizing the Confidence God Offers

### TRICIA LOTT WILLIFORD

A NavPress resource published in alliance
with Tyndale House Publishers, Inc.

# NAVPRESS⬤®

NavPress is the publishing ministry of The Navigators, an international Christian organization and leader in personal spiritual development. NavPress is committed to helping people grow spiritually and enjoy lives of meaning and hope through personal and group resources that are biblically rooted, culturally relevant, and highly practical.

**For more information, visit www.NavPress.com.**

22   21   20   19   18   17
6    5    4    3    2

*To Peter—*

*You are my sun, my moon, and all my stars.*

E. E. CUMMINGS, *73 POEMS*

*To Confident Girls—*

*may we know them,*

*may we be them,*

*may we raise them.*

# Contents

ACKNOWLEDGMENTS *ix*

INTRODUCTION: *You Can Do This*
The Confident Girl Joins the Conversation *xi*

1: *The First Bully of My Life*
The Confident Girl Knows Her Story *1*

2: *Wear Your Name Tag*
The Confident Girl Knows Her Identity *11*

3: *Write with Lipstick on the Bathroom Mirror*
The Confident Girl Appreciates Her Beauty *25*

4: *Claim Your Seat*
The Confident Girl Takes Her Place at the Smart Table *37*

5: *Plan Your Dinner Party*
The Confident Girl Doesn't Put the Critics in Charge *43*

6: *The Art of Dining Alone*
The Confident Girl Enjoys Her Own Company *57*

7: *Sex in a Box*
The Confident Girl Needs a Place to Put Her Stuff *61*

8: *Step Off the Merry-Go-Round*
The Confident Girl Feels How She Feels *71*

9: *Open Your Hands When a Gift Comes Along*
The Confident Girl Can Receive *77*

10: *Share Your Kindness*
The Confident Girl Sprinkles Kindness Like Confetti *93*

11: *Carry a Sharpie in Your Pocket*
   The Confident Girl Sets Boundaries  105

12: *Never Drop the Same Plate Twice in a Row*
   The Confident Girl Is a Confident Mom  119

13: *Be Where You Are*
   The Confident Girl Is Present and Engaged  129

14: *Wait for the Timer to Beep*
   The Confident Girl Doesn't Overreact  141

15: *The Underbelly of Confidence*
   The Confident Girl Chooses Vulnerability  147

16: *Put Fear in the Backseat*
   The Confident Girl Refuses Fear  163

17: *When You Feel Overlooked*
   The Confident Girl Can Hope  175

18: *Pass Your Brave Along*
   The Confident Girl Instills Confidence in Others  187

19: *Go and Be*
   The Confident Girl Is Ready  193

EPILOGUE: *A Joyful Commissioning*
   The Confident Girl Can Do This  197

GREAT BOOKS FOR THE CONFIDENT GIRL  *201*

NOTES  *202*

# Acknowledgments

SOME DAYS, writing is like climbing the side of a mountain; other days, it's like sledding down the other side. I am unspeakably and forever thankful to the people who help me carry my sled back to the top, who keep me in the game.

I thank my agent, Greg Johnson, who champions my writing and carries my words where they could never venture on their own. Greg holds the map for the journey, and he leads my way.

I thank the tremendous team at NavPress and especially Caitlyn Carlson, my editor, who is essentially a human Instagram filter for words. She says, "I see what you're trying to do here, and may I add a few things to sharpen the focus a bit?" And then she does her magic, and *everything* is more beautiful. My creative work needs help being born, and she is a most excellent midwife.

I thank my mom, who has been my first reader since the earliest days when I wrote sentences with crayon. She's still reading all of my sentences anytime I ask, making them stronger with her questions, suggestions, and refills of Diet Coke. She is my best-kept secret, the wordsmith in my pocket, and the keeper of the dreams.

I thank my dad, who decided on the day he became a father that his children would never, ever wonder whether he loved them. To this day, there has never been a question. My earliest confidence took root in very fertile soil and unconditional love. The world needs more dads like mine.

I thank my sons, Tucker and Tyler, who are the cream in my coffee, the ice in my Diet Coke, the sunshine in my clouds, the icing on my cupcake, and the laughter in my days. Guys, may you grow to lead and love, to recognize truth when you see it, and to know confidence as your own. You are smart and strong and mine, and I'm crazy about you.

I thank Peter, whose love and laughter are making me the best I've ever, ever been. Here's to singing in the car and dancing in the kitchen while days become years and moments become a life together. You are my heart's song.

I thank Starbucks once again, this time for letting me join your choreography behind the counter and begin the next chapter of my life. Take heart, baristas: You never know who will walk in the door.

And I thank the sea of readers, the invisible you who join me in these pages and on my blog, who let my story blend with yours. You keep me writing.

# You Can Do This

## The Confident Girl Joins the Conversation

*The clock is ticking, and the world is spinning, and we simply do not have time anymore to think so small.*

ELIZABETH GILBERT, *BIG MAGIC*

*You know what is really, powerfully sexy? A sense of humor. A taste for adventure. A healthy glow. Hips to grab on to. Openness. Confidence. Humility. Appetite. Intuition. . . . Presence. A quick wit. . . . A storyteller. A genius. A doctor. A new mother. A woman who realizes how beautiful she is.*

COURTNEY E. MARTIN, *PERFECT GIRLS, STARVING DAUGHTERS*

*I have complete confidence, O God;*
*I will sing and praise you!*

PSALM 57:7, GNT

**HERE. COME AND SIT WITH ME.** I've got a nice spot reserved for us here at my table, with a vase of daisies and my favorite coffee mug—the red one with white polka dots. Pour whatever you choose into your cup; it's not actually about the coffee, anyway. It's mostly about the warmth, the comfort, something to sip as we talk and think. Personally, I love my little polka-dotted cup for how it feels in my hands. I always feel more sophisticated when I am holding a coffee cup, and I find it helpful for gesturing, if you want the honest truth. And I hope we can agree that polka dots are almost always a nice touch. Polka dots and daisies are the essence of happy. Most of life is a little happier with a splash of one or the other.

Here's a little plate of caramel toffee scones, but don't worry—I didn't bake them. I mean, it's not like you should fear for your life if I offer you my home-baked somethings. I only say, "Don't worry" because I don't want you to think this whole scene is something it isn't: meant to impress or make you feel like I have it all together. It's just a table of intentional invitation. Because we're friends now, you and I, and I have a couple of things to say to you.

Let's start with an invitation: I'd like to invite you to stop being unhappy with yourself. To stop wishing you looked like someone else, or that people liked you as much as they like someone else, or that you could get the attention of people who hurt you. I'd like to invite you to stop second-guessing all of your decisions and commitments, to stop wondering whether your life would be different had you only chosen the mystery prize behind door number two.

I'm writing to you working moms who think you're not

doing enough to be present at home, and to you stay-at-home moms—to those of you who are unapologetically content at home and worry about getting things right in your long days with the little people who hold your heart, and to the ones among us who miss working outside the home and feel like they lost their confidence somewhere among crumbs and dirty diapers. I'm thinking of you single women who feel incomplete or not enough because you're not married. I'm writing to you single moms who balance more than you were ever meant to carry alone, and to you women who live with a failure, a betrayal, or a loss that has stolen every bit of who you thought you were.

I am inviting all of you, all of us, to a new conversation. I'd love to invite you to stop hating your body, your face, your figure, your hair, your freckles (or lack of them), your personality, your quirks. You're worth more than these self-imposed opinions. It doesn't matter when you began torturing yourself with criticism, but it needs to stop today. And here's what I'd love to convince you of right here, right now:

## *You can do this.*

Now, when I say, "You can do this," I'm afraid you'll call to mind clichés that I hate, the one at the top of the list being the lie that God won't give you more than you can handle. Not true. He will, and he often does. I could have titled this book *You Can't Actually Do This, but God Can If*

*You'll Trust Him with the Journey and Believe All Confidence Is Miraculously from Him, So Get on Board Because He's Better at Everything Already and What You're Doing without Him Is a Waste of Time and Energy.* But that's a little cumbersome.

So before we go any further—before we get to understanding how God has actually already offered us this confidence that we may not think we deserve—we need to face this one thing head-on: God will never give you a challenge or a limitation just because he believes you're strong enough to handle it. I've met so many women—and have often been one of them—who have been lectured into the lie that this challenge, this physical limitation, this disease or cancer, this crippling addiction, this loved one who's dying, this wondering-how-I'll-feed-my-children-next-week, and on and on, is a compliment from God. As if it's a job promotion. As if she has done so well with all of life's normal responsibilities that she's now been promoted to carry the heaviest things that come with life's hardest seasons, all because God thinks she can handle it. God doesn't work that way. He's not waiting to see how much we can carry before we are crushed under the weight. My goodness, I'm thankful this is not the God we serve.

While you may be facing a situation, a role, or a season right now that has caused you to believe you can't do it at all, you are not left alone in this journey. And the truth is, you *can* do this with the *real* truths in your pocket.

## YOU WERE MADE FOR ALL THE THINGS

I read some time ago about a woman who begins each day with a simple prayer: *God, let me be the answer to someone's prayer today. Guide my path, that I will cross theirs. And whatever you put before me today, I promise to do my very best.*

I love that prayer. I love it so much that I began to claim it too—this idea that God is right with me in all my moments, that he is working with me to make the most of every opportunity. And sometimes it's easy to live from that place. I have awaited God's plan for my days, and sometimes I have been abundantly aware of his direction in moments that can only be divinely planned, inspired, and orchestrated. I have belonged to conversations, moments, and encounters that were wholly destined. In praying these words, I began to await divine adventure, bigger plans, moments I couldn't have created on my own. On some days, he has handed them to me.

But some days hold no such moments. Some days, what God places before me is a list of menial tasks: endlessly washing sippy cups, answering Mommy-Mommy-Mommys, folding laundry, cutting coupons, planning menus, monitoring time-outs, adjusting attitudes, forcing naps on exhausted children who insist they aren't tired, teaching how to share, and acting as referee to boys who wish to be neither divided nor conquered. Some days, God places before me a call to love, joy, peace, patience, kindness, goodness, and faithfulness, all on one harried trip to the grocery store. Some days, he calls me to be the backstage manager who minds the cues and the curtain with quiet faithfulness, loving others and watching their dreams unfold.

I don't know about you, but it's not so easy for me to feel a sense of purpose when there's nothing shiny, sparkly, or even appreciated about the task at all. The lie we can so easily believe is that our small days don't matter—that sure, God might be with us, but he's not really doing much with us. But girls, hear me on this: We need to stop thinking that if we're not living up to grand expectations in our families, our jobs, our churches, and even ourselves, then we're not good enough. On those days when we think we are doing something small and insignificant, God has something big in mind. Some days, this business of the backstage and the sidelines and the unexpected is exactly where he wants us to be. And we need to have the confidence to step forward and claim who God made us to be, regardless of what fills our days.

Dear sister of mine, you were never intended to be walked on, degraded, disrespected, bullied, or belittled. God created Eve because he knew the world needed women. And not just to prepare meals like Betty Crocker, keep houses like Martha Stewart, be celebrity sex kittens in the bedroom, or make babies like machines. We may be good at some of these, and some of us are good at all of these. But it's not *all* that we are, girls. You were made because you matter, and you were never intended to live a life that matters less than anyone else's.

Somewhere along the way, we have become anxious and afraid, convinced that other people—women and men alike—matter more and are better equipped to face the messes of life. We are shying away from the paths in front of us because we are terrified we won't do it well, do it right, or do it enough. The most beautiful thing a woman can have is confidence, but as a culture, we're starved for a dose of it.

I'd like to tell you something you may have never heard, so lean in closely:

*You have the same goodness within you as all the people who you think are better than you.*

The only difference between you and a confident person is this one thing: confidence. We're all working with the same basic ingredients except for a handful of game changers, such as how you feel about yourself; what you tell yourself; and whether you believe God is in you, beside you, and equipping you to do this. God is the king of love, and with him we lack no good thing. The same power that raised Jesus from the dead is alive in me—and in you. It's a tremendous shift of security to realize that any confidence I have in myself is ultimately confidence in the one who made me.

## BEFORE WE BEGIN

Dear reader, with all due respect and affection, I need to tell you this before we begin: I didn't write this book to help you.

I have definitely written it *to you* and certainly *for you* to read, but I did not write it *to help you.* I wrote this book because I wanted to think about my own confidence. How did I find Confidence? How did she come to be mine? I wrote this book so that I can read it again later when Confidence has left me behind. She seems to hang out only with the prettiest girl at the party, and I rarely feel like I'm that girl. I wrote this book so I can remember later how to win her back. I wrote this book to remind myself whom God made when he made me, so another woman might embrace who he made when he made her.

And because I've written this book *to* you and *for* me, I'd love for you to join me, right here at my kitchen table. That's why I put the daisies in the vase and got the scones out of the bag and created this whole situation in the sunshine today. It's because I'd like to invite you into the confidence conversation. These words here are a chat between you and me, a dialogue about our confidence. The black parts are what I think, and the white space is for you and your thoughts.

To give space for your side of the conversation, I've included some rest stops along the way, at the end of each chapter. These include questions, points for further reflection or discussion, ideas for prayer, suggested exercises, and even some spiritual disciplines. I hope you'll let yourself slow down, engage your confidence on a deeper level, and respond. Add to what I've written. Underline what resonates with you. Respond with your own thoughts and experiences. Write in the margins. Make it yours. Coauthor with me.

Then, one day, if I ever have the pleasure of meeting you in person, we can talk about what we've created together. After all, you'll be the one who added the other half of the dialogue, the one who finished what I started. Join me in what God is doing here. I've found that anything he's part of is never, ever wasted time.

When you've finished reading this book, I hope you'll think, *This book made me think and laugh, and now I feel like I can do this next thing in front of me.* I hope you'll feel hope, courage, strength, encouragement, presence, freedom, and confidence to move forward into your life with the awareness that you were born for this. I hope, girl to girl and eye to eye, we can remember that we are called to claim complete confidence.[1]

Finding your confidence is a miracle. I know this because I found mine. And when I looked hard at the woman I've become, when I finally recognized the courageous warrior hidden in this frame, I was surprised by joy and astonished by awe. I want the same awareness for you.

Join me, girlfriend. Let's do this.

# CHAPTER 1

# The First Bully of My Life

## The Confident Girl Knows Her Story

*I wish I'd known from the beginning that I was born a strong woman.*
*What a difference it would have made! I wish I'd known that I was born*
*a courageous woman; I've spent so much of my life cowering. How many*
*conversations would I not only have started but finished if I had known*
*I possessed a warrior's heart? I wish I'd known that I'd been born to take*
*on the world; I wouldn't have run from it for so long, but run to it with*
*open arms.*

SARAH BAN BREATHNACH, *SOMETHING MORE*

**THE FIRST BULLY OF MY LIFE** was my fourth-grade teacher. My teacher, whom we will call Mrs. Wretched, seemed about eighty-nine years old; she wore polyester skirts and sensible shoes, and the flesh of her arms swayed when she wrote in cursive on the board. In what I can only assume was a grand gesture to avoid favoritism, she made sure none of her students felt liked or even acceptable at all. She yelled at children who looked out the window. Children who tattled on their classmates were sentenced to wear the Tattletale Name Tag. Children who leaned back on the rear legs of their chairs were banished to stand in humiliation for the rest of the day. There were rumors of dunce caps and noses held to the chalkboard. She probably had a box of stolen kittens in the bottom drawer of her desk. In my memory, she had warts on her face and a long pointy chin and a dog that she kept in a basket on the back of her bicycle. I'll agree to *perhaps* a very slim and remote possibility that she's become a caricature in my memory; but the truth is that Mrs. Wretched was legendary, and she was my introduction into the deep, dark waters of public education.

I had spent my first few school years in the sheltered, careful environment of a private school until my parents moved our family into the upper-class suburbia of their own hometown. To be clear, I wasn't transitioning to school in a foreign country, and the transition wasn't exactly culture shock. In fact, I would join the ranks at the same elementary school my parents had both attended in Greensburg, Ohio.

But I was an anxious little girl, and I felt like I had been thrown to the wolves. I was wildly nervous about the unknowns of a new building, a new lunchtime protocol, the location of the restrooms, this business of having a "locker," and what I should wear since red plaid uniforms were not the public school plan. My concerns numbered in the dozens, and it was all so new and so much for a nine-year-old girl who resisted change even on a predictable day.

On the first day of school, I stepped off the school bus

into a sea of kids just like me. I found Room 8 in the fourth-grade hallway, and I walked into my new classroom with the smile I had practiced. The other children were sitting impossibly silent at their desks, and Mrs. Wretched sat behind her desk at the far side of the room. With a flat tone and a firm brow, she barked at me: "Name. Bus number."

I deflated. I felt my fragile assurance slipping right out the toes of my new shoes. "Tricia. Sixteen."

"Find your seat and your locker."

I walked the row of lockers and found my name—misspelled as *Trisha*. I navigated the metal handle and put my bag on the hook inside the locker, quietly ignoring that Mrs. Wretched had spelled my name wrong. See, the thing was, I had never met another Tricia (or Trisha), and it turned out there were two others in my new grade, and one in this very classroom. I had made a grievous error in my first four minutes of fourth grade, but I didn't know it yet. A few minutes later, *Trisha* arrived to find someone's stuff in her locker. She went to Mrs. Wretched like Baby Bear complaining that someone's been eating his porridge.

Mrs. Wretched, who almost never came out from behind the fortress of her desk, walked over to Trisha's locker to retrieve my contraband: a Rainbow Brite backpack hung in the wrong place. "Whose backpack is this?" she demanded.

I raised my hand so silently, so subtly, just wanting to disappear.

She said, "The first thing you will learn in fourth grade is to respect other people's space. *That* is *not* your locker."

"But it said 'Trisha.'"

"And is that how you spell your name?"

"No, it isn't—"

"Well, do you *know* how to spell your name?"

"Yes, I—"

"You're not the only person in this world with your name, young lady."

She held my backpack hooked on her finger and waited for me to come and get it. I put it in my locker and returned to my seat, and I felt tears coming, coming, coming. I didn't want to cry. I just wanted a do-over. But you so rarely get a do-over on anything in life, and this was my first hard lesson in that truth.

I checked the name tag on the locker every day of that school year, terrified to make the same mistake twice. The locker was mine all year long, but every day I made sure.

Mrs. Wretched and I had a rough start to our year together, and it was hard to recover from that. As the first days lined up to become the first month, I found a routine in my new environment, but sadly very little improved. I had always loved school, but now my favorite parts of the day were any chances I found to leave the classroom. Recess, music, gym, art—I craved any opportunity for a break from her watchful, witchlike gaze. She was mean, and her unkindness stood out as the blatant opposite of the teachers I had had to that point in my young life. I had fallen so in love with my second-grade teacher that I had outlined my own career path to become a teacher just like her, and my third-grade teacher had named me her "little author" and wooed me into writing. I aimed to please, and my kind teachers rewarded my efforts with smiles and kindness. After love affairs with my earliest teachers, it never occurred to me that not every educator loves her job—that perhaps they wouldn't all love me.

Early in the fall, our school celebrated Right to Read Week. It was a nerdy version of spirit week, with daily themes such as "Choose Your Favorite Punctuation!" or "Be an Adverb!" or "Dress Like Your Favorite Person from American History!" For the last one, I chose Betsy Ross, and my costume became a family project. On that day, I went to school in a long, blue colonial dress, my curly hair swept up in a bun, and I even carried a picnic basket with an American flag carefully peeking out from under its lid. I mean, really, it was indisputable: I was a very charming Betsy Ross. Whatever you're picturing isn't nearly cute enough.

I started the day with my confidence restored. I had even packed an extra outfit for gym class—such was my preparedness. I'm pretty sure I said to myself, *I've so got this*, or whatever was the equivalent circa 1988. I stopped by Mrs. Wretched's desk, and I asked her, "Where should I put my clothes for gym class today?"

In retrospect, I knew the answer to that question. Of course any extra items of mine would go in my locker. But I think I wanted to give her the chance to be overjoyed by my costume. I probably pictured in my mind a scene similar to Ralphie's dream in the classic movie *A Christmas Story*, when his teacher reads through so much drivel until she finds his paper: finally one worth reading, the work of a student who has restored her faith in education and her very self. In other words, I set myself up to inevitably see firsthand how very unimpressed she was.

"I don't even know why you're dressed like this," she said. I took a step back, feeling shoved away by her disgust.

"Because it's American History Day," I said, my voice wavering.

"*That* is tomorrow. Now go change your clothes."

I carried my American flag, my picnic basket, my extra clothes, and my nine-year-old dignity down the hall to the bathroom, trying to decide what to do with it all. I pulled the pins out of my bun and shook my hair free. I stuffed my colonial dress into the basket, I changed into a very plain T-shirt and pair of jeans, and I gave myself a few minutes to just cry.

I just wanted to move forward, to go on with the day, to somehow get out of the crosshairs. But when I came back to the classroom, even though I tried to will myself to be invisible, she noticed I had been crying.

"Crying again, I see," she said, with an exasperated sigh. And then, loud enough for everyone to hear, "Tricia, I have never in my life met a child with less confidence than you. I certainly hope you grow up to have more confidence as an adult, because you are a child with none."

Who does that? Who says that to a child? I was devastated. I didn't know what the word *confidence* meant. I didn't know what it was. But when I was nine years old, an adult told me I didn't have any of it. And when an adult slaps a label on your chest, it sticks.

Have you ever had someone like that in your life? Someone who threatened to steal the spirit right out of your soul, the joy right out of your smile? It's sadly and likely true that you have a story similar to mine. Someone who stole your confidence right out of your pocket. Think about it. Let's do a little detective work to think about who did this to you.

These thieves are probably the voices you still hear in your head when you're right on the edge of doing something really creative, profound, brave, or simply joyful. If you're like me, maybe you hear objections in your head: "You think you're creative? Since when? When is the last time you had an idea that was actually yours, or worse, actually *good*?" Or "Who do you think you are, trying to do something so brave? Leave that to the people with real courage. You're just faking it." Or "Somebody sure thinks highly of herself, doesn't she? Stop bragging. Don't you realize how prideful that is? That's not humility." Or "You're an impostor. You might as well wave the white flag and give up, or else somebody's going to blow the whistle on this little charade you've got going on. And I think we can agree it will be far less painful if you surrender on your own before somebody makes you."

Were those words painful to read? They were painful to write. I get it, my friend. Where do those voices come from in your life? Parents? Teachers? Coaches? Siblings? Bullies your own age or, as in my life, significantly older? How about an old boyfriend? Or maybe even the person you're married to today? Maybe it's something even bigger, something without a face or a voice, something harder to identify—like the culture of your church or the religious beliefs of your family. Sometimes we get to a point in our lives when we realize that what the "grown-ups" have been telling us the Bible says isn't actually in there at all. Sometimes grace gets lost in criticism, and self-worth gets swept away with rules.

Look back on the stages of your life—childhood, adolescence, college, early jobs, careers, marriage, motherhood, successes, failures, and the transitions in between—and think of the people who influenced you. Think about who walked with you on these journeys, and think of their voices. What did they say to you? Did they build you up or tear you down—give you life or drain you like a helium balloon with a slow leak? If these voices come into your head when you think of the worst things you believe about yourself, then my friend, you've found the thieves of your confidence. Their passing comments plant the seeds in a fertile ground of negative thoughts, and before we know it, those seeds grow into oak trees of personal beliefs.

Negative thoughts and beliefs are just that: thoughts and beliefs. They are not facts, and they do not need to be true. Each one of these holds you in bondage, and each one must be shut down. You are not ridiculous, overly emotional, selfish, or grandiose just because somebody said you are. What you are is terrified.

That's the thing about negative thoughts and beliefs: They keep you scared. You're afraid of getting hurt, afraid of being seen, afraid of being shamed or shut down for not measuring up to the rest of the world. And these thoughts are ruthless. They will search until they find your most vulnerable place: your beauty, your lovability, your intelligence, your sexuality, your courage. When criticism finds vulnerability, it grabs on tight. Before we know it, we are bound tightly in the tentacles of an octopus that's very much in charge. Girls, we very simply and truly and deeply *cannot let those thoughts be in charge of us*. We can get our confidence back from the thieves who stole it from us. We can choose a different way.

## Stepping Forward

Think about the time when your confidence was stolen from you. Jot down the details that come back to you—who said it, how he or she looked at you, the room you were in, the way you felt, and how your parents responded if you talked about it. It's so important to acknowledge the ways we've been hurt and the things that have been taken from us, because here's the thing about wounds: They almost never go away on their own. They only create thick scar tissue that keeps us from being real, authentic, brave, or confident. Write down what you remember about the ways your confidence has been taken.

Set a timer for twenty minutes and journal about what you wrote down. Lean into the pain instead of avoiding the memory. The infection is there; see if it will come out when exposed to the light of day.

In the same way, think about a time when you have stolen confidence from someone under your influence. Is there something you may have said to your husband, your sibling, or your child in a harsh moment of stress or exhaustion? If a memory comes to mind, it may have stayed in that person's mind, too. A conversation and a request for forgiveness can restore the relationship as well as the very confidence that was stolen away.

Do something nice to reward yourself for all this emotional heavy lifting you've done today. You have been brave, you are valuable, and you deserve kindness—first of all, from yourself.

# CHAPTER 2

# Wear Your Name Tag

*The Confident Girl Knows Her Identity*

*To do good things in the world, first you must know who you are and what gives meaning in your life.*

PAULA P. BROWNLEE

**THERE'S A LEGEND** I love about Ernest Hemingway. Folklore says that he was in a restaurant when someone challenged him to write a story in only six words. If I were a betting girl, I would have sided with the men at the bar, believing it was impossible to have plot, character, and conflict in only six words. But Hemingway won the bet with this short story: "For sale, baby shoes, never worn."

(I've always found that so haunting and captivating. I really want to know who's selling those shoes and why. Well played, Hemingway. Well played.)

*SMITH Magazine* began collecting six-word memoirs a few years ago, and these memoirs have become something of a literary phenomenon. Anyone can give it a try—writers of any age and stage, skill, and ability. People all over the world began thinking in six-word increments and submitting their stories.

Isn't everything really a short story? The story of this day. The story of this week. A poem, a sentence. Even a novel—isn't it the weaving together of several short stories? If I can write one good short story, then maybe I can write another, until they become a beautiful collection: the story of a woman, a family, a life.

If I'm actually living a short story, and if you are too, then perhaps all of life is actually the weaving together of a million short stories into one epic page-turner. God is the ultimate storyteller. He's been writing a story since the beginning of time, and it continues for all eternity. The first words of the Bible say, "In the beginning," and that really means "Once upon a time."

It's an interesting exercise to think about your life as a six-word memoir. What would it be? What six words would summarize any seasons or truths about your life?

May I tell you a few of my own?

I was in second grade when I decided I was going to be a teacher. As a seven-year-old curly girl, I set my mind on a future with a classroom of my own, and I followed a careful and strategic path to teaching full-time. High school, college, practicums, student teaching, licensure testing, interviews, and finally a job.

There are a few things in life that are so blessedly formulaic. Recipes. Algebra. Chemistry. Certain career paths.

Put together factors, ingredients, and timing; follow the steps; mix it all together; and lo and behold, you have what you're looking for. Some things are like that. Other things are not quite so predictable and linear. Love. Joy. Parenting. A career as an artist. Potty training. But the path to becoming a teacher? One specific choice after another. Sometimes the pieces of your story fall right into place, just as the formula promised.

When I became a teacher, I defined myself as one. I thought like a teacher, and I began collecting the things I believed teachers should collect. (There was a strong and pervasive apple theme. My life was one giant apple orchard.) I dressed like a teacher, right down to the plaid jumpers and wooden jewelry. (I'm not proud of the fashion sense in that season of my life. We all make terrible decisions we'll live to regret, and as we live and learn, we can only hope nobody will post proof on Facebook.) All of this to say, I was a teacher, inside and out, and I defined myself largely by that role.

Perhaps my six-word memoir for this stage may have been *Life is like a lesson plan.*

Or *Always crafting my next bulletin board.*

Or *Teaching the next generation to read.*

In that same season of chasing down my role as a teacher, I met and fell in love with my husband, Robb. I was twenty years old when I married him, and I leaned into my role as a wife. My wardrobe was pretty consumed with the apple and wooden-jewelry theme, so I can't say it really affected my clothing choices; but I pursued the role of "wife" with the same kind of intensity. I collected books, conversations, and mentors—I looked everywhere for people and resources who would teach me how to do this. (Apparently I learn by immersion.)

Perhaps my six-word memoir for this stage may have been *I look twelve in wedding photos.*

Or *Crock-pots are a bride's best friend.*

When my children were born, I stepped out of the classroom and claimed my role as mom. This one called for some serious rethinking and personal redefinition. I was still a "teacher," so to speak, although I had a classroom of two children instead of thirty. I had been a spontaneous extrovert, and I was now bound by routines and nap times and board books. I began to redefine myself as a homemaker, since it was right there in front of me, day after livelong day. I had to come to terms with what I liked and did not like about this job—and let's just say that there is still much I don't like and much I am not good at. I love the role; I don't love the tasks.

Perhaps my six-word memoir for this stage may have been *Goldfish crackers. Board books. All day.*

Or *Again with the laundry and cooking?*

Or *Can it be nap time now?*

To balance what I didn't love, I started leaning into writing and editing, exploring the skills and income I could bring to the table through writing and freelance editing while my toddlers were sleeping. My roles and definitions were clear, measured, and safe. And that was just the way I liked them.

That worked well until a morning in 2010, when Robb died. I'm sorry for how quickly and abruptly I turned that corner with you, but that's how it happened: quickly and abruptly. He was sick for only twelve hours before he died. He was healthy and then he was sick; he was here and then he was gone. I was thirty-one years old, my children were five and three, and suddenly my world was torn apart. Overnight, I became a widow. I was a lost, frightened, traumatized, unmarried bride. I became the single mom of two small boys who were now fatherless. I could no longer think as a teacher, writer, or editor; my brain was consumed with the tasks of getting out of bed and fighting depression and posttraumatic stress with every ounce of my being. Sometimes the pieces of your story fall into place, and sometimes they fall apart.

Perhaps my six-word memoir for this dark season may have been *How on earth did this happen?*

Or *Widowed mom, trying to wake up.*

Or *Winter, winter, winter, winter. No spring.*

Or *I wasn't ready to say good-bye.*

Or *I still have things to say.*

I had lived inside clear, measured, and timely definitions. I planned my days and followed basic six-word maps that said, "Start here, arrive there. All done." In twelve terrible hours, my roles changed. My definitions became unclear. I felt like the entire world had tilted on its axis by about thirty degrees. So much looked the same, but nothing felt right. And the new path was not linear, not defined, and certainly not safe. So much of my identity felt suddenly and terribly missing.

Few events foster such a fertile petri dish for insecurity more than a deep, sudden loss. My loss was my husband, but perhaps you know a loss of a different kind. Perhaps divorce—a death all its own, coupled with crippling rejection. Or the loss of a job, the loss of a friendship, a loss of respect, a loss of innocence. Confidence is fragile and fleeting, and it scatters into the darkness of what is unknown and unavoidable. We each have our stories; "each heart knows its own bitterness."[1] Sometimes life is impossibly hard, and this world is the scariest place to be when you no longer know who you are.

Careful, intentional definitions feel safe because they're known. Sometimes a person can get deeply caught up in *what* she is instead of *who* she is. When one's identity is defined by *what* she is, then she can find herself thrown off-kilter and spinning into orbit when those nouns change. We become like Russian nesting dolls, with layers of our core hidden inside other versions of ourselves. We become our definitions. Even if these definitions are no longer true, they feel safe and comfortable, like protective layers.

This was true of my wedding rings. Since nobody gets to tell a widow when to take off her rings, I wore mine for months after Robb died. In my heart, I was married, and I desperately wanted to keep the identity that the world gives to a bride with a ring on her left hand. I remember looking down one day to see that two of the baguette diamonds had fallen out, like missing teeth. Part of me wanted to rush to the jewelry store and get it fixed, as if fixing the diamonds would somehow fix the whole broken story. But another part of me, the part of me that felt forever broken, truly identified with the gaps of those missing diamonds. Somehow the sparkling, shining, tattered, and broken parallel made perfect sense.

I took off my wedding rings when I knew the time had come. Wearing them no longer felt like truth. It felt like a memory. It felt like the last threads of something I was holding too tightly. I felt like I was pretending to be a wife. So I took them off and put them away; then I got them out; then I put them away. Because that's how it is when you're finding a new identity: Sometimes you find yourself putting the old one back on again, just to see if it still fits. It was a long time before I could take them off and tuck them safely and permanently away: a reminder of who I once was but no longer a banner I needed to wear.

Definitions are like that. Even if they're not a good fit anymore, even if you outgrow them, even if your interests have shifted or your life stage has changed, perhaps you are still holding on to a definition that is no longer true simply *because* it's comfortable. Maybe you wish it were still true. Or perhaps the opposite has happened: You believe your definition might still be true, but maybe it's becoming a little uncomfortable.

The hardest definitions can be those that other people put on us. Nobody knew that more than the women of Jesus' time. Women interacted with Jesus in some pretty important

17

and surprising ways, and the Bible is teeming with the stories of the women he spent his time with, the women he ministered to, and the women he spoke of in his parables. They were the first at the foot of the cross and the last to leave. They were the first to speak of his resurrection. They were valid witnesses to the truths of Jesus.

This was especially significant because women received so little respect in that day. They were slaves, children, or property. They were considered unclean and prohibited from worshiping in parts of the Temple. They lived a lifetime of "less than." But Jesus arrived on the scene with a new regime and a new definition.

Jesus was a storyteller, which is naturally one of my favorite things about him. He could paint an exquisite word picture. A third of his teaching happened in story form—and he revolutionized the culture for women by simply including them in his stories.

He taught about the obstinate widow and the harsh judge. She asks and asks and asks and asks. Finally, the judge says yes. The lesson of the story is to pray persistently, and the hero in the story is the persistent woman who embraces humility and asks for what she needs. She—not the judge—is the hero.[2]

He taught about the woman who lost her coin, who searches her entire house until she finds it. The lesson tells of Jesus' heart for the lost, that he'll turn the world upside down to find the one who needs him. And in this story, of all things, he presents a woman as an analogy *for himself.*[3]

And imagine how his words must have sounded when he told the parable of the leaven and dough. He said, "The kingdom of heaven is like yeast that a woman mixed into a large amount of flour until the yeast worked its way through all the dough."[4] Guess who was making the bread in their everyday culture? The women. So imagine how this resonated with the women in the audience, who were so accustomed to hearing stories they couldn't identify with and teaching that didn't relate to their experiences at all. Suddenly, Jesus talked about their daily tasks—kneading yeast into the dough—as an analogy of his Kingdom. He spoke their language. He came into their world, and he said, "I see you. I see what you are doing with the hard work of your hands, these tasks that go unnoticed by the end of the day. I see you and I know you. You matter to me."

Jesus used stories like these to show his feelings, thoughts, and attitudes about women. But his elevation of women didn't stop there: He also encountered many women, face to face, whose real-life stories are now written into the Bible. He talked to and about women in some brand-new ways, giving them value and worth that they'd never known before.

There was the woman who had been bleeding for years and years and who touched Jesus' robe, believing in faith that she might be healed, even if he never noticed her frail existence. He upheld her for her faith—he let her touch him. And yes, she was instantly healed. Not only did her bleeding stop immediately, but she also could now be restored to her place in her family, her church, and her society. She was no longer unclean. Jesus gave her life back to her.[5]

Then there was the widow whose son had died, which meant the end of her life—if not physically, then certainly financially. Nobody would care for her; she would be reduced to poverty and begging for scraps. Jesus met the funeral procession, touched her son, and resurrected him. Everyone around him believed that Jesus had defiled himself, but he didn't care. He resurrected her son and—my favorite part—said to her, "Don't cry."[6] The thing about an imperative statement like that one is that it sounds so bossy, but I really don't imagine that Jesus spoke to her with a bossy tone. I imagine he was so gentle with her. That maybe he held her, let her rest against his chest, and maybe even stroked her cheek. I imagine that he very gently said to her, "Dear one, don't cry."

And we've all heard the classic dichotomy of women, Martha and Mary: those who are filled with busyness, and those who are filled with rest. Martha seems so distracted, needing to serve, busy, and occupied—she forgot to be attentive. All the while, her sister was still, worshipful, and in the presence of the Lord. We've always noticed that Jesus honored Mary and rebuked Martha, reminding Martha to be more like her sister. But the truth is that Jesus honored Martha because he saw that she was teachable. He stopped his conversation, focused on her, and taught her a lesson in an age when rabbis did not teach women. Jesus stopped her, saw her, and taught her. This was revolutionary.[7]

And since John in his Gospel tells us there were many

more stories of all that Jesus did, I imagine that Jesus talked to many, many women. He touched them. He taught them. He welcomed them. He invited them to worship, and he showed them how. He changed everything through his teaching, his attitudes, his miracles. He reached out to women, and he allowed them to know him. He ignored men's views of women, and he disregarded rabbinical rules, tossing them to the side because they just didn't matter to him. Instead of looking past women as an entirely invisible population, he said about each one of them—and now each one of us—"I see you. You matter to me. You are welcome here. Just come to me. Worship me. I want you, and I'm inviting you to worship me. Just come to me. I love you."

If anything stirs a woman's heart, it's that kind of invitation. Our hearts soften when we are welcomed into someone else's. So often, our safe and comfortable definitions offer us the very opposite of what we're seeking: Instead of giving security and a sense of belonging, these definitions leave us feeling outcast, alone, like we don't belong. Jesus' definition of us throws the door wide open and says, "You are worthy and loved, and you belong."

If we boil it down to the most basic definition, I think confidence is the belief that there is a place for you. This search for belonging runs rampant on the first day of middle school, when we're looking for a table in the lunchroom. Those cafeteria memories (and smells) are so fresh in my mind, so easy to recall. I remember walking through the lunch line, carrying my tray, and hoping to quickly and silently find a place to sit before anyone could smell my fear. If I'm honest, there's a part of me that will always be a middle schooler navigating the cafeteria of life, hoping to quickly find my place; dodge the microscopes of critics; and feel known, seen, and safe. If you're like me, you know that fear of rejection stays and grows with us, and it seems to always come down to the same question: Is there room for me at this table?

At this dinner table?

At the conference room table?

At the Communion table with Jesus?

When you believe there is room for you at the table, then you move forward with careful confidence. You know there is a place for you.

So what defines you as a woman? Is there a six-word memoir you are holding on to as your identity?

- *Wishing someone could call me Mom.*
- *I'm the family's Big Screw-Up.*
- *Climbing corporate ladder. Hit glass ceiling.*
- *I really thought I loved him.*
- *I really thought he loved me.*
- *Credit cards maxed. Nothing else left.*
- *Looking for love on dating sites.*
- *Bathroom trips are my only solitude.*
- *Living the dream I didn't want.*

- *This diagnosis will swallow me whole.*
- *I'm a cake—everybody wants pieces.*
- *This loneliness is now my life.*

But what if Jesus, our ultimate storyteller, were to write your six-word memoir? Maybe it would look something like these.

- *You are mine; you are enough.*
- *You: beautiful, cherished, seen, known, loved.*
- *You are welcome here, beside me.*

Here's what you can know for sure, beyond the shadow of doubt, no matter how you feel from day to day and moment to moment. God knows your name; you belong to him.[8] He sees your every move, and there's no place you can go where he won't join you.[9] He thinks about you, and he smiles over the idea of you.[10] He is with you wherever you go.[11] He will fight for you,[12] and he has a plan for you.[13] He is good,[14] he is freedom,[15] and he has a place for you: next to him.[16]

Wear your name tag and know your identity, my friend. There's a place for you here.

## Stepping Forward

I truly and simply love six-word memoirs. I've doodled them in the margins of journals, on airport cocktail napkins, and even in a library book or two. (No, that's not a typo. It really was a library book.) Though I must warn you: Once you start reading six-word memoirs—or writing them—it becomes addicting. You'll find yourself thinking in phrases that match multiples of three for a long time to come. What are your six-word memoirs?

If Jesus were to send you a very personal message that speaks to your fears of rejection or loss and to your questions of who you are and where you have a place, what might he say? What six-word memoir might Jesus write about you?

Think forward in your imagination by twenty or thirty years. What six-word memoir do you want to describe you then—the inner you, the woman you hope to become, the legacy you want to leave? What memoir do you hope someone else might write about you at that point in time? Set out to make it true.

# CHAPTER 3

# Write with Lipstick on the Bathroom Mirror

### The Confident Girl Appreciates Her Beauty

*You can never be too well read or too inspired. (Who cares about thin and rich!)*
JANET FITCH, FROM THE FOREWORD TO *A WRITER'S BOOK OF DAYS*

*Pretty women wonder where my secret lies.*
*I'm not cute or built to suit a fashion model's size.*
*But when I start to tell them,*
*They think I'm telling lies.*
*I say,*
*It's in the reach of my arms,*
*The span of my hips,*
*The stride of my step,*
*The curl of my lips.*
*I'm a woman*
*Phenomenally.*
*Phenomenal woman,*
*That's me.*
MAYA ANGELOU, "PHENOMENAL WOMAN"

A PERFECT PAIR OF JEANS IS one of the best things in life; shopping for the perfect pair of jeans is one of the worst things in life. That whole shopping situation is a bittersweet lesser of two evils, don't you think? I do love me a good pair of jeans, and when I find them, I wear them until the threads between my thighs wear so thin that it's no longer appropriate nor fixable with duct tape. And then my heart breaks, and I finally throw them away with a more grievous and emotional send-off than I've given to some of my children's pets. That's when I realize I have no choice but to start anew.

My search for just the right pair has led me across the path of many low-rise jeans. (Here is where I extend a very sarcastic thank-you to all the pop-star-models of the world who have made a two-inch zipper the new norm. No, really. Thank you for this ridiculosity.) I would not consider myself to be overly modest, and yet one would think I am the only woman in America who does not want her entire middle (and lower) region revealed to all the world. Now, I do happen to believe that appropriate clothing changes with age and life stages. For example, a teenage girl might dress differently than one who is in college. And a single girl might dress differently than one who is married. I am married with children, and that calls for a different degree of propriety than my single, sorority-belonging sisters. I have finally begun to embrace the "classic rise." I do realize that the name implies a pair that rises above my belly button, perhaps in the category of "mom jeans." But I assure you, this is not the case. I love trendy jeans as much as the next girl. It's just that what was once labeled "sits below waist" in the olden days is now "classic rise." *Sheesh.*

The words *skinny* or *boyfriend* don't usually work for me in the jeans realm. I need words like *curvy* and *flare.* And if they could work in the word *forgiving,* I'd be a customer for life. I forever struggle with the measurement situation of having both a waist *and* hips. If the jeans fit around my gracious bigger parts, then they don't fit around my precious smaller parts.

Recently when on a mission to find jeans, I went into a store I love and trust. Because I need to go to places I love and trust if I'm going to put myself through the body-image gauntlet. I found a curvy pair of flare jeans, but when I looked on the rack, I found only sizes 0 and 00. Oh, forevermore.

(Let me just say here that those sizes should not be allowed to exist since we don't accept zeros—let alone a double-zero—in any other kind of measurement. On the clothing racks, women are motivated to shrink down to a number that anywhere else means *nothing, no value,* and *invisible worth.* It's time to reevaluate our sizing system.)

I asked a sales associate for some help. She was the cutest, most elfin creature I had ever seen. I said, "I think these might be the very perfect pair of jeans I've been searching for my whole life, but do you have this style available in any other sizes?"

She reached up on her tippy toes to look at the sizes available. "Oh, how funny that these little tiny sizes are all we have!"

Yes, so funny. And not at all awkward. I could barely contain myself over the overwhelming hilarity of it all.

In an attempt to mask my vulnerability in asking the darling elf for help, I said, "Right, because I am looking for, like, *people* sizes. Not so much doll clothes."

"I know, right? These are actually the size I wear," she said, at which point the whole scene got exponentially worse. Until she said, "My brother always teases me that I could sleep in a dresser drawer when I come home to visit," at which point I felt straight-up Amazonian.

"Yes, well, you are kind of pocket sized," I said. "I've always thought that must be so nice."

"Oh, I haven't always been. I was probably three or four sizes bigger than this just a few years ago."

So during your "bigger years," you were a size four? I'm pretty sure you and I don't order off the same menus in life, from appetizers to opportunities.

And then I had to tell her what size I needed in these maybe-perfect jeans, which felt too much like needing to tell my doctor my embarrassing symptoms in hopes of getting a prescription to make it all better. She started a fitting room for me, and I followed her pert little self down the little hall, believing once again that the world belongs to the small and thin, to those whose bodies make sense to them. The rest of us must make sense of things on our own.

⁊◌

For a brief season of their childhood, my boys gave gymnastics a try. In retrospect, I think they were more interested in learning fancy trampoline tricks, but nonetheless, for a few months I spent many an afternoon in the tumbling gym. My mind wandered while my boys were flipping and flying with the one class of little boy monkeys in a room full of ballerinas and gymnasts. It was a microcosm of the hierarchies of body image.

There is the preschool class, the little girls who are brand-new to tumbling and somersaults. They have such sweet lines, round tummies, and the pockets of sugar that can be found only on a little girl who still wears a princess nightgown to bed. Then there are the elementary-age girls, and they could be here for any of many reasons, not the least of which is social. Gymnastics and athletics may or may not be on the agenda. A few shine as future Olympians, and the rest flip and giggle and adjust their ponytails. The older groups contain girls who are serious, who have muscles in their thighs and their upper arms. They have a dusting of white powder on their hands, and they walk with grace and authority. (I'm pretty sure they own the room at any pool party.)

One sweet little gymnast flips and turns, walking her body backward, hands over feet. Probably nine years old, she is long and lean, her blonde hair pulled into a loose ponytail with flyaway wisps held loosely by an orange barrette that matches her team uniform leotard. Her movements are graceful. Her body is her own.

I hope for her that she will come to know herself before her body is no longer in her favor. Because it will not always be. For now, she flips and turns with the ease of a falling leaf, with a similar carefree breeze. But there were so many shapes and sizes in that room, and I wanted her—each of them—to know that beauty doesn't look one way. My heart went out to the girl who was shaped more like the number 8 than the letter *I*. I wanted to give her a tube of red lipstick so she could write across her bathroom mirror, "I am crazy beautiful."

We have a hard time loving our own brand of beauty sometimes, don't we? It's not our fault, this disgust we've come to believe is just part of looking in the mirror. We all know we're targeted for every kind of marketing comparison, and this body-image branding starts younger and younger. In an effort to swim against the current and not be swept away, I wanted to learn to see myself correctly, to remind myself of what God made me to be. I wrote a letter to myself, about myself. I titled it "My Compliments to My Creator":

*Dear Most Magnificent Creator,*

*You have made heaven and earth, everything in and on it.*
*You called it good.*
*You make all things glorious and for your glory, and*
*you made me.*
*This can only mean that you have made me good,*
*glorious, and for your glory.*
*My compliments to how you made me, Master Artist.*
*Thank you for my curly mane, wild and unruly,*
*that waves in the wind and gets bigger in the rain.*
*Thank you for my hands, patterned after my dad,*
*with long lean fingers.*

*Thank you for my fingernails, my greatest vanity,*
*forever manicured as the splash of color against*
*everything I make with my hands.*
*Thank you for my middle, for the waist of a woman*
*and the soft belly of a mom.*
*Thank you for my legs, which I graciously use for*
*sitting crisscross as I comfortably read and write in the*
*corner of my couch, and not so much for running.*
*Thank you for hips, for curves I want to appreciate.*
*Thank you for collarbones, which I believe to be the*
*most beautiful part of any woman.*
*Thank you for making my body to be healthy,*
*sturdy, feminine, and strong. You made me good,*
*glorious, and for your glory.*
*My compliments to you, now and forevermore.*

Girls, I might as well be naked before you right now for the degree of vulnerability I'm feeling after having written that down. Until now, it was just between God and me, safely hidden on the bound pages of my journal. But I want you to see the gentle gift I gave to myself, this handwritten love note about my physicality, this awareness that I'm not less because my measurements are more.

If God is like any artist I know, which is likely since we are made in his image, then maybe it matters to God when we notice what he has made. When we can agree, "You made that for me, and I like what you did. Thank you."

૭✦ා

I was doing yoga in my bedroom. And by the way, you haven't lived until you've tried to chaturanga with a child tickling the back of your knees. Or do the downward dog with a child trying to limbo underneath you. Or do the chair pose with a child trying to use you as an actual chair. All while they're peppering you with questions such as "Why does God make us worship him? And why is our pee yellow?" It's like yoga on steroids. And there's no namaste about it.

Anyway, I was in a mountain pose when somebody spotted a stretch mark on an inch of my exposed waist.

"Mommy, is that your birthmark?"

"Nope, that's from when you were growing inside me. My skin was being stretched in so many directions when you were growing, so those streaks and stripes happened."

"Did it feel like those pains in my feet that happen at night?"

His puppy paws are growing into these great big feet, and sometimes we have to ice them at night because the muscles ache from growing so fast.

"Yes, I think it might be like that."

I have my share of silvery stripes across my middle. Four pregnancies and two C-sections later, my wrinkled, puckered tummy looks like a "dried apricot," as my friend L. once said. It's true. But you know what? I love my stretch marks. They tell a story. They are victory scars. When I look at those stripes across my abdomen, I remember when my children were growing inside me, when they were just mine, when they went everywhere with me, and when only I knew when they had the hiccups.

And when I look at the six-inch scar from my C-sections, I think of the moments I met them, when I first heard them cry, when I watched them meet their daddy for the first time in the operating room. I think about how amazing it is, an everyday miracle, and how blessed I am that God let me participate in bringing them into the world. He could have chosen to do it all without my involvement.

Recently, I saw a bottle of Stretch Mark Eraser on display at the mall, professing to take those stripes away with some faithful moisturizing. I didn't even pause to pick it up. First of all, I don't think it would really work. But more importantly, I don't want these marks to go away. Why would we want to remove the telltale signs of the privilege of giving birth to another individual? So that we can impress someone who sees those lines as some sort of flaw? I'm not sure I could become genuine friends with that person anyway, so I'm not interested in shaping or erasing any part of my life to get his or her attention.

I feel the same way about wrinkles. I remember the day, in the first year after Robb died, when I looked in the mirror and realized that my eyes looked older. My spirit was aging, and the skin around my eyes had begun to wrinkle and crinkle like crepe paper. I wasn't yet thirty-two; I felt too young to feel so old, but I didn't even care about the wrinkles. They were bound to happen sometime. I remember thinking I'd rather give my youth to a broken heart than hand it over to sun damage. Wrinkles mean you have loved, gray hair means you have cared, and scars mean you have lived. Why in the world would any of us want the rest of us to think that we have reached the ripe age of (insert yours) without ever really living?

Anyway, my son was not so sure. He studied my dried apricot, and he said, "I would hate to be a girl."

"Well, there's a lot of work to being a girl, that's for sure."

"Yeah, like getting cut open to have babies."

"Well, there are some good things to being a girl too."

His brother chimed in, "Yeah, like your bathrooms are so much nicer."

"Mommy! That's so true! Who needs fluffy chairs in public bathrooms? Girls, I guess."

His brother joined him with this conclusion: "I think it's so they can sit there and make sure everybody washes their hands." (Yep, gentlemen, this is the very definition of womanhood: yoga pants and stretch marks and overstuffed chairs in the bathrooms. Plain and simple, you could say these are the trade-offs we get in exchange for the fact that you guys get to pee standing up.)

Listen, I'm all about being healthy. (Well, I'm not *all* about it. I'm actually much less about it than I am about other things. Like ice cream.) But let's remember the difference between wanting to be healthy and needing compliments on how good we look. If your workout center is wallpapered in mirrors, have you paused for a moment to consider why that might be? It's not for admiring one another's integrity and character. I want to be around women who look deeper into themselves instead of longer at their reflections. I am drawn to the women who admire one another for the richness of their life experiences and the wisdom they've earned, for the scars in their stories and the stretch marks on their spirits, for the strength of their hearts and the depth of their thoughts. I long for the days when we can each do that for the woman standing next to us.

Let's start rejoicing in the bodies we have because that's a true and honest way of looking more deeply into ourselves. We are the creations that God made and called good. God said to Peter, "Do not call anything impure that God has made clean" (Acts 10:15). There you have it: permission (and instruction!) to choose this day to love the way you're made.

*P.S. I found my pair of jeans, and they are a good fit, albeit classic in their rise and flaring in their legs. But finding them was a long, arduous process, and the three-way mirrors were not kind. I'm asking Jesus to come back before I wear these out.*

## Stepping Forward

Write a letter to yourself and about yourself, quite probably only for yourself. Title it "My Compliments to My Creator." Tell yourself everything you like about you, everything you were born with that's beautiful. Include a list of the scars you are most proud of. Maybe it matters a lot to God that you notice what he made.

I remember reading somewhere, "Beautiful young people are accidents of nature. Beautiful old people are works of art." Consider the women you truly admire. Why do you admire them? Is it because they are in their sixties but still look not a day over twenty-two? Why is that admirable? List the qualities that make older women beautiful. Let these be your timeless priority, not the ticking clock of agelessness.

Do a favor for the women you meet along the way: Compliment them on something that looks beautiful about them, right that moment. Maybe you only notice that the shade of blue she's wearing brings out the blue in her eyes; tell her. Maybe you wonder to yourself how she doesn't just topple right over on those tiny, delicate feet; tell her. Or maybe you notice that she had little time to devote to her appearance today; she's simply working her way up the produce aisle with a baby on one hip and a five-year-old helping her push the cart, and she's being so patient with both. Tell her she's wonderfully patient and a beautiful mom. Perhaps for a moment today, each of those women will believe you, and maybe they'll smile. And a smile always makes a woman all the more beautiful.

# CHAPTER 4

# Claim Your Seat

*The Confident Girl Takes Her Place at the Smart Table*

*There is something you must always remember. You are braver than you believe, stronger than you seem, and smarter than you think.*

CHRISTOPHER ROBIN, *POOH'S GRAND ADVENTURE*

**SOMETIMES WHEN I'M ABOUT TO** tell a story that feels intensely personal, I think of telling it as a fairy tale instead. "Once upon a time, there was a girl." It just seems a teensy bit safer to create that kind of dissociation, to offer just an inch or two of distance between the person in the story and me.

But I'm the person in the story, and it grows monotonous to refer to myself as "the girl." So, whatever. Here you have it. All my cards and dirty laundry.

When Robb and I started dating, back when I was nineteen and he was twenty-three and my friends were so impressed with what a man he was—with a full-time job and a salary!—I created a pattern that turned out to be unhealthy. I affirmed his every word, declaring him to be the smartest man I knew, the keeper of all information, and knowledgeable in all things.

"You know everything," I would say to him, with a hazy, love-struck gaze. (Even now that makes me nauseated. I seriously can't stand to be around girls like that.)

A friend even said to me, "You know that he doesn't, right? You do actually *know* that he doesn't truly know everything?"

"Well, sure I do. But what is the harm in stroking his ego? What's the harm in showing him I'm impressed with his intelligence? Is there anything wrong with affirming the things he says, agreeing with him, and learning from him?"

Well, no. There's not really anything wrong with that at all. Except that's not what was happening. And *that* became the problem. Robb was a very intelligent man with lots of knowledge, to be sure. But all of my babbling about his super-genius IQ didn't do either of us any favors.

First, even though I didn't mean to, I put Robb on a pedestal he couldn't maintain. He didn't want to let me down or mar the image I had painted, so he became inordinately afraid of saying "I don't know"—after all, his lovely bride had declared that yes, of course, he really did know all things.

He became a secret keeper, a vault of information, somehow convinced that if he let me in on everything he knew, I'd find him less attractive, less charming, less knight-like. So he stopped telling me things. The risk of showing all his cards felt too much like saying, "That's all I've got. I know no more. I'm not who you think I am."

Worst of all, I depicted myself inaccurately. By declaring

him all-knowing, I acted as if I knew little, as if my intelligence were lacking, as if I were simply blessed beyond measure because he had bestowed a portion of his wealth of knowledge upon me.

I'm a smart girl. But something in that twenty-year-old bride believed I would be more attractive if I weren't quite so smart. I think I believed it would intimidate him if I could keep up, so I pretended as if I couldn't.

We were married for years before we began to unveil this delusion, and by then some patterns were in place that neither of us wanted. We had to retrain ourselves to say, "I don't know" and "I think I do know." Each brings its own humility. We worked hard to find clarity, to claim the vulnerability we had surrendered with those early mistakes in the name of flirting.

Later, as I entered the dating scene again, now with a lot of years and miles on my widowed frame, I was appalled to find myself stepping into the same patterns all over again. I remember being on a date with someone who would eventually pass through my life, and as I affirmed his knowledge and intelligence on whatever topic was his expertise, he began to think I knew nothing. And alarms sounded in my head.

I love smart women. I really, really do. I have surrounded myself with them in my social circle, I have been known to pursue friendships based solely on my desire for the influence of another woman's intelligence, and I truly value a smart girl with a bright mind and a quick wit. I kind of get high on intelligent conversations. So here's what I would love to know: When did it become socially acceptable (or even desirable) to be a woman who is not smart?

Last week I had lunch with an old friend who took every opportunity to degrade herself and her intelligence. This is a girl who has pursued a professional career, completed postgraduate work, and established a life of independence based on her intelligence. Somehow, she believed she was more approachable, more desirable, and perhaps even more lovable if she marked herself as less intelligent than the average girl. In a very tactful, diplomatic way, I called her out on it. It's bunk. She's a smart girl; why pretend otherwise?

I also learned recently of another very smart friend of mine being ridiculed in a circle of women. They teased her for having a degree, for being an eloquent writer, and even for using "big words." She left that girls' night feeling degraded and minimized, all because she is a smart woman.

And how is it possible that pop culture is filled with smart women wanting to appear stupid? They are clearly bright enough to market themselves with a slant one way or the other, so why not capitalize on their intelligence? I can list fewer than five openly "smart women" in today's entertainment world. Please tell me: Where have all the smart girls gone?

I am the last to say that a woman needs credentials, degrees, or titles to prove she is smart. I have very few of those myself. I have high aspirations for all of them, but I'm a smart girl without any initials after my name. And I know it. You'll never hear me say otherwise.

My mom is a brilliant, wise, confident woman. She is no less feminine because she can keep up with any man, and my dad loves her for it. In our home, there was no excuse for pretending to be something I was not. I could not claim inadequacy when we all knew I could do it. (Except in sports. Everyone knew I couldn't.) I have held fast to the value I have learned since I was small: Know who you are, be confident in what you do, and never say you can't when you can. Don't let anyone put you in a corner because you're a girl. Know your stuff and do it right.

I don't have a daughter, but if I ever do, I suspect this may be our greatest challenge in raising her in a culture that minimizes women. I will give my everything to teach her to value everything about herself, especially her intelligence. I think women the world over are forever making up for the first time a woman said, "Oh, dear man. You are my hero because you are so much smarter than I am." I raise my glass to the smart girls. It takes serious guts to be one.

So, once upon a time, there was a girl. She'd like to do it differently this time.

## Stepping Forward

Find something you're passionate about and dive into it. Choose something you want to know more about. Read a book, take a class, listen to a podcast. Learn about it. Even master it. Do you know why? Because you're smart.

Do you surround yourself with people who treat you as though you are not as smart as they are? Change your surroundings. Everyone is smarter about something than you are; you're smarter than they are about something else. Don't let their self-proclaimed brilliance get way out of proportion in your mind.

Write a list of what your very own mind does especially well. Are you great with numbers, or better with words? A whiz at puzzles? Do you have an astounding memory for names of people you meet? Do you sense the meaning behind others' words? Has your mind made it possible for you to paint, sew, or otherwise create beautiful things? Can you sense when others are troubled, when most people wouldn't notice? See? You're a smart girl with a strong, amazing mind. Don't let anyone tell you otherwise.

# CHAPTER 5

# *Plan Your Dinner Party*

## *The Confident Girl Doesn't Put the Critics in Charge*

*No one can make you feel inferior without your consent.*

ELEANOR ROOSEVELT

**IF THERE'S ANYTHING** I can do well, it's dinner parties. I am genetically predisposed to them, having come from a long line of hostesses who can throw a party at a moment's notice with zero stress or concern. This happy tradition fell by the wayside in my dark years of grief, when Robb's death stole all my desire and energy for being with people, let alone hosting them. But when the sun began to shine again, two of the best things that came to life were my menus and my dishes. You know my emotional health is intact when a dinner party is in the works.

I love the conversation, the energy, the music, and the hospitality of it all. If I'm hosting a party, there will undoubtedly be too much food. That's intentional, and the reason behind it is this: If there's only one dinner roll left, then you might feel hesitant to take it. On a grander scale, and more importantly, you might feel like an unwelcome afterthought, as if I didn't plan for you when I invited all these people. And I simply won't have that. So I'll freeze or share the leftovers, but by George, plenteous food will abound.

I give a passing glance to the details, since I do believe that's where love and intentionality live, but I absolutely straight-up *refuse* to get stressed out. I embrace the grace that says every home should have a secret room, the place where you can shove your stuff and close the door so you can plan a party on short notice and let the guests in without any embarrassment. Maybe you are a better homemaker than I, and maybe you don't need such a room. But I like that I can just put things in that room, close the door, and party on. Embrace the grace, people.

I plan the menu, invite the guests, and then move forward with the belief in my heart that the rest of it will come together. And it will indeed come together if you keep this in mind: Your guests must truly mean more to you than the perfection of the home you invite them into. If your purpose is to get gold stars for the amazing color scheme and the unadulterated absence of dust in your home, they'll sense it. But if you desire for them to feel so comfortable and at ease in your home that they can laugh—or cry—with abandon, then you're on to the secret of genuine hospitality.

I am convinced that the heart of a dinner party boils down to two nonnegotiable components: place cards and conversation questions. It's not the food that makes the party; it's the people and the conversation. I create a place card for each person, because a place card says, "I want you to be here. See? I wrote your name with my pretty pens because you matter, and I knew you were coming, and there's a place for you at my table."

On the back of each card is a conversation question. Because here's the other thing: I despise small talk. De-*spise*. You've been there: locked in a social conversation where no one is talking about anything of value but talk has to happen so that no one feels awkward, and so mouths keep moving and conversations drift through lukewarm waters. Cocktail parties exhaust me because I hate fluttering about and never really landing. I am just selfish and insecure enough to hate knowing there's probably a better conversation happening in this room, and I'm not in it yet, so I'd better keep moving until I find the best and most intriguing dialogue. Just thinking about that makes me tired, so I'd rather stay home in my jammies. But when I'm planning the party, there is no way I want my guests wishing they were home watching Netflix. So I bring all the guests together over one really good question. Then the introverts can rest and listen, the extroverts can think out loud, and I can rest assured that I'm not missing the heartbeat of the party.

There you have it—all my hostessing secrets. You're welcome.

Here is my favorite dinner party question: "Who's invited to your dinner party? Of all the people in all of the world— living or dead, past or present, famous or everyday—who do you want at the table?" This makes for great conversation, I promise you. You can learn a lot about your guests by learning whom they aspire to host. My guest list always includes authors and actors, writers and artists, thinkers and leaders. Ultimately, they're the ones I admire up close and from afar, the current voices I'm letting into my life.

For a ladies night, I would invite Elizabeth Berg, Anne Lamott, Marisa de los Santos, Maya Angelou, Elizabeth Gilbert, Jamie Lee Curtis, Nora Ephron, Jen Hatmaker, Julia Roberts, Oprah, and my mom. I would serve a buffet of appetizers and sparkling beverages on a table the color of limes and tangerines. I've got it all figured out.

For a night with the gentlemen, I'd choose Tom Hanks, Steven Spielberg, Aaron Sorkin, Andy Stanley, Brennan Manning, Donald Miller, Jimmy Fallon, Abraham Lincoln, my brother, my dad, and certainly Peter, who is funniest in living rooms (I'll tell you more about Peter later on). I would serve bacon-wrapped filets and beer, and we would have after-dinner conversation coupled with a coffee bar. (Wait. Do men do coffee bars? Maybe a cigar situation of some kind. Stay tuned.)

The reason I'm giving you these two guest lists in such detail is that it turns out that the dinner party guest list has actually become an important filter in my life.

℘

A few years ago, a political magazine approached me to write for them. They said, "Trish, we love your writing voice. Our readers are mostly men between the ages of forty-five and sixty-five, and we want their wives and daughters to read our magazine. Your voice is young and fresh and fun, and we want to hire you as a columnist."

Young, fresh, and fun? Well. That really is quite a pickup line, I have to admit.

There was just one very obvious problem. I said, "But you're a political magazine. I am apolitical." Here's why I am apolitical: because I am not competitive and I don't like arguing. In political conversations, tensions run high and there always seems to be a winner and a loser. These are not my ingredients for fun and enjoyable things I like to return to.

But the political editors said, "That's what we love about you. You'll mix it up a bit with your apolitical voice. Please write for us."

When you're an artist and someone likes your work, you're complimented and flattered and boosted by the idea that maybe you've fooled them into thinking you know what you're doing. When you're a starving artist and someone offers to pay you for what they like, you say yes even if you don't know what you're doing. So I said yes. I put my toe into the waters of a whole different genre, and I got quite an education.

See, what I didn't know was this: While I was writing to attract the wives and daughters of their readers, I'd have to contend with the angry husbands and fathers who came to argue. People signed on to the site from their left and right political agendas, and they came to defend their side.

Instead they found a charming little article about single parenting in the suburbs, or an encouraging word to moms who can't think of a dinner plan that doesn't involve Cheerios, or a harmless little anecdote about the day my child locked me in a second-story bedroom. (This episode involved tying sheets together to wave out the window, screaming for help to strangers, and finding my toddler in drag.) They hadn't signed on to read charm and encouragement and harmlessness. They came to be polarized and political. My writing was a serious disappointment.

So they'd read my stuff, and then they would *rip me apart* in the comments section. Under their anonymous screen names, they were unbelievably mean. They said things such as "You're feeding your children trash, and you deserve to eat trash."

Or "A woman so stupid to raise her children this way doesn't deserve to have them."

Or "You single moms deserve no honor. You get what you get for lying down in the first place with a piece-of-trash man."

Or "What an idiot. If I were you, Tricia, I wouldn't put my name on this kind of stupidity."

Or, quite unbelievably, "Your Satanic rant is filth. Join the ones like you in hell."

Or, the most wounding, "Of course someone is going to write this garbage, and of course it would be Tricia Lott Williford. You can't trust or believe or credit anything she writes."

What is it about the comments section that so perfectly distills humanity down to our most despicable and vile form?

Seriously. I had agreed to write simple, happy essays about slices of life, but I had thrown myself to the wolves for a paycheck.

I was like a little girl dropped off in the big city. I had grown quite accustomed to writing my small-town stuff for a small-town audience. Even though they were all over the world, they belonged to me and I belonged to them. I told them my stories, and they told me theirs. We signed on each day to find one another on the screen, and they knew my words were true and real, just like me. So they were kind to me. I would give them my thoughts, and in exchange they gave me kindness. It was a good gig, a mutual outpouring of words and kindness. When I jumped into the deep end of editorial journalism, I wasn't yet skilled in posting-but-not-reading-the-comments. I didn't know the thick skin of the political world. And frankly, I didn't want to grow the thick skin required to make it there.

I have to tell you, those kinds of attacks take a toll. No matter how much I promised myself I wouldn't read the comments, no matter how much I told myself that the angry trolls were likely sitting in their underwear in a dark basement, eating Doritos and scrolling through online forums, I couldn't dismiss their voices. I became more and more cautious with my writing, until my articles were sterile and impersonal. I stopped telling stories about my life, I shared nothing about my family, and submitting an article felt comparable to sneaking up on the neighbor's big, slobbering, sleeping dog, poking him with a stick, and then running away before he could catch my scent. (Except that my name was written in the byline, so my scent was easy to track.) My best days were those when I posted an article that nobody noticed. When I wrote something that nobody read, I felt like I had slipped under the radar. Which isn't really the point of writing, by the way. But I was tired of dodging bullets and tired of hiding from bullies.

Here's the worst part of it all: I stopped writing. Even though my blog was alive and my readers were still gracious and kind and waiting for me to contribute to our conversation, I felt afraid to say anything anymore. A few times, the angry readers from the political magazine found their way to my blog—or to my personal e-mail—and they began to spew their venom in forums that had always been safe. I felt like a terrorist had moved into my neighborhood. My writing pulse grew faint along with my courage, and I got really quiet. The bullies and trolls of the Internet won the battle; they had silenced me.

In my writing silence, I read voraciously. I took in books and articles and blogs in giant gulps. Reading is breathing, and I was starved for fresh air. It's a mysterious thing that happens, but I love how books find me. I read *The Guernsey Literary and Potato Peel Pie Society*, and my favorite line in the whole book is this: "Perhaps there is some secret sort of homing instinct in books that brings them to their perfect readers. How delightful if that were true."[1] This idea enchants me to no end, and I believe there must be some measure of truth to it. I don't know how it works, but it does. Books find me when I need them. In my writing silence, the words of other writers found me.

Glennon Doyle Melton was the first to speak. I affectionately call her G (I write a swirling capital G next to every quote of hers in my journals, and they are many—both her quotes and the journals). G and I don't agree on everything, but I will always and forever want to have her over for dinner so we can drink Diet Coke out of wine glasses (because it really does taste better that way). Glennon wrote a blog post in response to a writer who was ready to give up. The exhausted writer spoke my very words: "The criticism is what's getting to me. It feels like every time I put myself out there—every time I show my heart—somebody criticizes it. And I just feel tired." Um, yes. That. Everything *that*.

Glennon's response was like a tall glass of water to my heart:

Here is the problem. Here is why you are so tired and you want to quit: *You are doing more jobs than the jobs you have as an artist.* . . .

You write a beautiful, you-filled piece—you *create*. Then you post it—you *give it to the world*. So far so good.

*But actually . . . you don't really give it. You don't release it.*

You hang around your art. You follow it around and make sure everyone is being nice to it. . . . You become your art's lawyer, or its babysitter, or maybe its secret service agent. THAT is what's making you

tired. Because you are not a lawyer or babysitter
or armed guard, you are an artist. You have taken
on too many jobs. . . . No wonder you're exhausted.[2]

I read that, and I breathed, "Yes." It wasn't a cheer or an
exclamation but an exhalation of relief. She was right. That
was what I had been doing: creating, putting my very heartbeat into everything I made so it could breathe on its own,
and then following it around to make sure the world didn't
knock the wind out of what I had made. On G's suggestion,
I thought maybe I could do all of this differently, following
the creation model of my Creator: Create. Call it good. Rest.

And then there was Brené, whom I lovingly and simply
call Brené because her name is magnificent enough to stand
on its own. In her book *Daring Greatly*, she said she had
learned that the people who love her, the people she really
depends on, were never the critics who were pointing at her
while she stumbled.

They weren't in the bleachers at all. They were
with me in the arena. Fighting for me and
with me.

Nothing has transformed my life more than
realizing that it's a waste of time to evaluate my
worthiness by weighing the reaction of the people
in the stands. The people who love me and will
be there regardless of the outcome are within
arm's reach. This realization changed everything.[3]

And then there was Oprah, one of the only names forever consistent on my imaginary dinner party list. I really want to have dinner with her, but not as an adoring fan. I want to be her friend. (Actually, I spent a good many years just wanting to be Gayle King, her actual best friend in real life.) I listened to a podcast in which Rob Bell interviewed Oprah, and she told about a time when she had called Maya Angelou, crying over some piece of untruth that a journalist had written about her in a tabloid. She cried on the phone to Maya Angelou because it was all so unfair, unkind, and untrue.

And then Maya said,

> Baby, you're not in it. You weren't in it when they sat down at the typewriter to write the story. He wasn't thinking about you. He was thinking about what's going to make the story. So it really doesn't have anything to do with you. And baby, those people cannot hold a candle to the light God already has shining on your face. Focus on the light. Focus on the light. Can't you see the light?[4]

When I listened to Oprah's story and Maya's wisdom, I was sitting at a table in Starbucks. I leaned back in my chair, and I looked out the window and right into the sun. I let Maya's words wash over me like a warm, rich blessing.

Here's the thing. I believe in the sisterhood of women. I think we are one of God's finest creations, a tapestry woven of the richest colors. We pour into one another in a beautiful blend of giving and taking, of speaking and listening, of cooking and dining, of twirling and standing still. I listened to the sisters who had paved the way for me—my mentors who don't know my name, but I sure know theirs.

At some point over my many hours with books lying open on the table before me, written by all of the above authors, I realized that in my own little way, I had kind of hosted one sparkling, fantastic dinner party. My favorite girls came: Glennon, Brené, Oprah, and even Maya Angelou. They dined with me, these strong matriarchs in the field I have chosen, and they filled my cup. I let their words wash over me. That's how it is at the best of dinner parties. You let the guests and the conversation and the food and greatness of it all swallow you whole.

Maybe that is actually a great filter for the voices of critics in your life: Would you want to invite them to your dinner party?

If you wouldn't give them a seat at your table, then don't give them a voice in your life. They're allowed to talk because everybody has the right to a voice. But darling, don't you know? Just because they talk doesn't mean you have to listen.

When I was ready, I began to write again. I picked up my pen, and I opened my computer. I poured some Diet Coke into a wine glass, I put on a fresh layer of shiny lip gloss, and I began to write. But I write differently now. I no longer follow my writing out into the world, and I don't let the trolls find their way to me. I simply set my writing free to explore the world, to live and breathe on her own, to wander into the hearts of the ones who need her. Just like the words of the sisterhood found me.

The confident girl is careful about whom she listens to, and she sure doesn't put the critics in charge. Not everybody gets a voice, and certainly not everybody gets a seat at the table. Choose wisely. And then bask in the goodness of your dinner party.

*P.S. If you're reading this and you found yourself on my guest list, feel free to shoot me your RSVP. We'll find a date that works. I'll also cook a killer meal and surround you with some charming dishes and sparkling conversation. Just sayin'.*

## Stepping Forward

Who is speaking into your life? Have you allowed the critics to somehow be in charge? Take back your spirit and put it in good hands. If they're not people you would invite to your dinner party, then they don't get a voice of criticism in your life. (And if the bullies in your life are people you have welcomed into your home, then it's time to set yourself free and set some boundaries. We'll talk about that in chapter 11.)

Girl, it's time to throw a dinner party for your favorite, safest people. Plan the menu, invite the guests, and then move forward with the belief that the rest of it will come together. Somehow, it always does. (Remember the place cards and conversation questions. This is where the goodness hides.) How many guests? Well, how many does your table hold? If you have room for a dinner party of four, then find three guests and you'll be good to go. And if a brunch or lunch party sounds more inviting to you than a dinner party, then go for it. That's part of the privilege of being the hostess.

Finally, here and now, let's make a pact—you and me and all of us—to disengage from participating in, or even reading, Internet arguments. These can be the ugliest, most venomous encounters with some of the most toxic behavior in the world. It's a coward's battleground where people are needlessly cruel behind the anonymity of screen names, and it's not good for anybody involved. Let's be better than that.

# CHAPTER 6

# The Art of Dining Alone

## The Confident Girl Enjoys Her Own Company

*You will realize that a little loneliness goes a long way in creating a richer, deeper, more vibrant and colorful you.*
MANDY HALE, *THE SINGLE WOMAN: LIFE, LOVE, AND A DASH OF SASS*

I NEVER INTENDED TO be single again, but I found myself in that place for more than five years. It goes without saying that I would never have wanted any of that to happen. (Like, for real, not *any of it.*) But as it often goes with the worst things, now I have learned the deep value of that season. I wouldn't trade that time of *quite quiet and alone* for a whole lot of seasons of *loud and crowd.* I learned more than I'll probably ever be able to fit into a lifetime of writing. On the list of greatest lessons: how to enjoy my own self.

Have you ever taken yourself out for dinner? Just you, all on your own? There was a time when I never would have considered it, a time when seeing someone alone at a table just broke my heart with sympathy for their loneliness. But I think differently about it now. I now know that *alone* doesn't mean *lonely*, and the person I felt so sorry for may not have been lonely at all. I contend that there's an art to dining alone, that it can be a beautiful and life-giving adventure to believe yourself to be quite enough to occupy a booth for two. So even if you have a regular dinner partner, I invite you to learn this skill when you have the occasional opportunity. Here we go.

The first thing to know about dining alone is this: It's all about you. So dress yourself right into a good mood because you're actually taking yourself on a date. I'm something of a podcast junkie, and one of my favorites is NPR's *Invisibilia*, a podcast about the invisible forces that control human behavior. In an episode called "The Secret Emotional Life of Clothes," Lulu Miller and Hanna Rosin explore how clothes can change us in quiet but surprising ways. Their research showed that our personalities shift when we feel confident in what we're wearing. Our clothes can even affect our intellect. Adam Galinsky, a professor at Columbia Business School, ran an experiment where he gave people a doctor's white coat to wear for a series of intellectual tests. He discovered that people tested measurably better when they wore the doctor's coat, simply because they *felt smarter*.[1] It's proven and measurable that your confidence, personality, and perception of yourself can be directly tied to what you're wearing. So why not get dolled up for a night with yourself?

Next, choose a place you love to go with food you love to eat. When the host says, "How many in your party?" be ready with your answer. I try not to say, "Just one," because tonight isn't about feeling sorry for myself, and the word *just* gives the wrong impression, making it sound as if I'm lonely and sad. Let's be honest—if I'm lonely and sad, then I won't need a host to seat me. The dinner by myself is going to look like ice cream in bed and *You've Got Mail* on Netflix. Instead, I say, "I'm dining alone tonight, thank you" or "A table for one, please." Those are proactive statements that put you in charge. It's your chance to say, "I chose this night, this restaurant, and this time by myself. Please give me the best table that will suit such a quality time and experience."

Bring a companion of some kind. I bring authors in their books. But maybe you bring apps, Angry Birds, singer/songwriters on Pandora, or your Facebook community on Words with Friends. I've spent many a "dinner alone" with Oprah or Brené Brown simply by bringing their words along, and Michael Bublé has been known to sing to me through my earbuds. Much as at your dinner party, you get to choose whom you're with—even when you're all alone. And though you look like you're having dinner by yourself, only you know that you're in the presence of quite fascinating company.

Next, choose your very favorite item on the menu. And this part is very, very, very important: Order dessert. Always. This is a must. You're worth it, and life is too short to overthink the cheesecake. Settle in. Leave a good tip. If you don't have the luxury of spending very much money on yourself, then treat yourself to dinner at a frozen yogurt shop. Enjoy the space. Love yourself there. It's an art, this business of dining alone.

Why is it important to get comfortable being by yourself? So that later, when someone comes along to fill the space beside you, you'll know for sure whether you're choosing to be with someone out of love or loneliness. These are very different, and only the girl who knows herself can implicitly learn the difference. Sometimes you have to be alone in order to find out who you are without anybody telling you. Sometimes you have to be alone so you can learn the sound of your own voice.

## Stepping Forward

Try some solo activities. Take a sketchbook to the park. Check out a new exhibit at the museum in your town, and dawdle at any display that interests you, since no one gets to hurry you along to *their* interests. Shop for something frivolous (I recommend a coffee mug that fits perfectly in your hand). Pamper yourself with a day at the spa. Catch a matinee movie, complete with popcorn. Quite simply, don't be afraid to be alone. There are some great perks to a night on your own: You don't have to agree on the movie genre, and you don't have to share the dessert. Enjoy your own company. You may be surprised to find that you're a most fascinating person to spend an evening with.

# CHAPTER 7

# Sex in a Box

## The Confident Girl Needs a Place to Put Her Stuff

*It doesn't happen all at once. You become. It takes a long time.*

MARGERY WILLIAMS, *THE VELVETEEN RABBIT*

"TRICIA, I WANT YOU TO create a box in your mind where we can put all your thoughts." Jana told me this one afternoon during my counseling session. If you've read my other books, then you've heard of Jana (whose name rhymes with Dana, not with Hannah). Jana is my therapist, and I've spent at least an hour a week with her for many, many years now. She has wisdom beyond measure, she makes killer muffins, she fixes stubborn carburetors, and she expects honesty from everyone—most certainly including me. She reads my every signal as plainly as words on a page, and it's a good thing I trust her with my very life because there's nowhere to hide under her watchful eye.

My therapy in Jana's office has evolved and changed with time over our last six years together. I came to her on a cold

January afternoon just a few weeks after Robb died, and I've seen her every single week since, barring her family's vacations or mine. A psychobabble cynic could make the argument that my hours in therapy have in fact paid for good portions of her family's vacations. To that, all I can say is this, with 100 percent certainty: I'd spend every one of those dollars again in exactly the same way. Jana is my lighthouse. She's worth her weight in gold and lattes.

When I came to her—dazed and absent, skeletal and broken—she counseled me, the grieving widow. More than a year later, the darkness had again shifted in my life; I had been deceived by a skilled manipulator who had taken advantage of my mind, my body, and the person I knew myself to be. Jana listened, studied me at an entirely different level, and then applied skilled therapy to me as the victim of a sexual predator. Grief therapy and sexual-assault therapy are two very different things, but she is masterful, I tell you.

All people have chapters of their lives they don't read out loud, Jana has taught me. Things happen with or without your consent, and sometimes you can't claim your confidence until you have owned—and been able to set aside— the stuff that got you where you are. Manipulation and abuse are mighty oppressors against a person's confidence. God is good and mighty to heal, and sometimes he uses the skills of therapists and the chemistry of antidepressants to get us on our feet again. Utilizing these is not weakness, only wisdom. If you need help, get it.

As the layers of trauma in my life unfolded in Jana's office, we embarked on a whole new process of trauma therapy called EMDR, or eye movement desensitization and reprocessing. It's a big name and a revolutionary science. Jana began guiding me through the neurological science of identifying the places in my body and my mind where trauma had gone to hide. She would teach me to set those memories free to be logical facts, not triggers for fight or flight. The thing about EMDR is that you gain a whole new level of access to your thoughts, but it's pretty dangerous to go there unsupervised. So she wanted me to practice putting it all away. That's when she asked me to create a box where I could put all my thoughts.

Immediately I was intrigued, in part because I have always loved a colorful project. I feel like my shining years as an artist were my masterpiece Valentine boxes in fourth and fifth grade. But I could also feel myself withdrawing a little bit, because she had just asked me to create something, and that requires imagining, and I don't really have much of an imagination. I'm a noticer, not an imaginer. If she had placed a box before me and asked me to describe it, I could have written some glorious sentences with metaphors so lovely they'd make you want to weep. But invent a box? Make one up? Both *from* and *for* my imagination? I don't know, Jana. I don't know about this at all.

She said, "This box is going to be the place that will contain everything that's overwhelming to you, the place where you will put everything away when it's time to stop thinking about it. You're a words girl. Tell me what this box could look like."

I looked at her blankly.

She said, "Okay, let me tell you about mine." She closed her eyes, visualizing, and told me about a gigantic wooden trunk with a lock and key that she had mentally buried in the sands of the Middle East, a place she was sure she would never, ever go. She opened her eyes to look at me, and she said, "It can be as big as you want, as far away as you want, anything you want. Just make sure it can hold everything you want to put in it."

"Okay, I'm tracking," I said. "I can picture that box."

"Great, so you've got the idea. Now tell me about yours."

"Well, I guess it's like yours." I offered to adjust the shape of my box, giving it a curved lid like a pirate's treasure chest with the rusted lock.

She said patiently, "Make up your own, please."

"But I liked yours."

"And you need to own your own."

I closed my eyes and took a deep breath, trying again. This time, I pictured a great big pot on a stove. In my mind, it was round enough to hug and thick enough to boil all the spaghetti for a whole Italian family's Sunday dinner. My great big pot sat on the back burner of the stove, out of the way of the other things I wanted to stir and create with my good energy and thoughts.

She said, "I like it. Tell me, what is the pot doing right now? What does it look like on the stove, while you're making other things in the kitchen?"

I opened my eyes. "Actually, it's boiling over."

"Well, then, that won't do, will it?" She smiled her Jana smile, the one that emerges any time I've come to the conclusion she was pointing me to without her needing to say it out loud.

My imagination had offered the very outpouring of my inner self. I seemed to believe that my wounds and worries were too big to be contained, that if I ever stopped thinking about them, they would boil right over into a big mess on my metaphorical stove and catch my whole life on fire.

"No, I guess that won't do."

I sat up straight, closed my eyes again, and took another deep breath, now determined to invent a box that was uniquely mine and somehow big enough to hold all my boiling, roiling mess. And then it came to me. I held out my hand, touching my palm with my pointer finger. "That's how big it is."

"Tell me more," she said.

I told her about this little round ceramic bowl, only big enough to hold a pair of earrings. In my mind, the lid opens with a hinge, and the clasp clicks when I snap it shut.

"Is it big enough?" she asked.

With my eyes closed, I plucked one giant apple off an imaginary troubling tree in front of me. My invisible apple shrank in my hand until it was the size of a pearl. I held it in two fingers and dropped it in the round bowl, listening to the clink of the pearl and the click of the clasp. Locked up tight.

I opened my eyes and met hers. "Yes, it's big enough,"

I said, "because I am bigger and stronger than the things that have happened to me. I have the power to shrink anything I want to put inside my pretty little box."

She winked. "Good girl."

My pretty little box holds more than I can list, and I return to the image of it often. I call on the pretty little box when I'm wide awake late at night, when my mind brings to the forefront every ugly thing I've ever seen up close and in real life. I pluck these images out of my mind, shrink them in my imagination, and drop them in the box and put them away.

I call forth the pretty little box even in the light of day sometimes, when fear and worries get ahead of me because I'm not living in today. I pluck words like *money* and *retirement* and *sickness* and *loneliness*—and many other such words on a broad spectrum of reality—and I drop them in the box, deciding I will get them out at a more appropriate time, should they ever manifest into actual real, living things that deserve my attention.

I always *pluck* the idea from my mind, *clink* it in the box, and *click* it shut. These little onomatopoeias remind me of the meaninglessness of fear, worry, and regret. It's always very satisfying to pluck them with such ease, then to hear them clink against the ceramic insides of the box, and then to close the clasp with an effortless click. Every time, I breathe a sigh of relief as I remember that imaginary, invisible things are not in charge of me. I am in charge of me.

❦

Now, let's take this concept and shift our focus a bit to add a new layer. As it turns out, a confident girl can have more than one box in her armory because this practice of imagery is a transferable skill. I have another box I've recently invented. I call it the Sex Box.

When Robb died, I was thirty-one years old, but try not to get sad about that right now because I'm not writing about anything nearly so deep as being widowed. No, instead I'm addressing the debatable science of a woman's sexual physiology in her midthirties. There's a hormonal peak that happens in this life stage as fertility begins to decline, and this time frame seems to be when women "want it" most. I've read that it's debatable, and I don't know if it's science or not, but I don't really operate on facts and research. Science, schmience.

The bottom line is this: I was as hormonal as a fourteen-year-old boy, and there are some perks Robb missed out on by going to heaven early. I missed sex.

But here's the real truth: More than the sex, I missed the intimacy. They're not the same thing. Some can put a price tag on sex; nobody can put a price tag on intimacy. You can't buy it, you can't sell it, you can't demand it, and you can't even give it away without someone to hold it for you. Giving intimacy to someone who doesn't want it is a shade of desperate self-disclosure, and it's not healthy. Intimacy is a gift. It's a recipe of knowing, learning, remembering, falling, catching, and keeping. That is what I missed.

I think we each have a limited number of intimacy dollars to spend before they're gone, before we will have nothing left to give when we would most like to make a sizeable investment in one person.

I made a few mistakes in my five years of unexpected singleness, mistaking counterfeit dollars for the real thing. These choices only left me feeling spent, brokenhearted, and desperately vulnerable. If the price is low, then the goods aren't worth much.

Sex isn't intimacy. And I was not willing to sacrifice one for the other. It would cost too much. It would steal from what I had with Robb, from what I would have again. I had to believe there was a man out there who believed sex is far more valuable than the cost of a dinner date (or two or three), who believed intimacy is a priceless, forever exchange. So I guess you could say that I started saving up. And I needed a place to put it all. Hence, the Sex Box.

The first box I invented on Jana's request was meant to hold anything I didn't want to deal with, anything I couldn't handle. This box, quite differently, was a place for the things I wanted (a lot . . . I wanted these things *a lot*), but they weren't yet mine to enjoy again. In my mind, this one is a large square box wrapped in beautiful white paper, tied with a red satin ribbon. With some careful placement of my thoughts, that box began to hold everything I longed for, everything I wanted to do, the gifts I hoped to someday give and receive, and every wandering thought that needed a place to go before it stirred up trouble I couldn't contain, before it wrote a check I couldn't cash.

❧

We've been all over the map so far in this chapter, from trauma therapy to sex and intimacy. Stay with me here, girls, because all these boxes lead to the same thing: The confident girl needs a place to put her stuff.

We all have stuff, don't we? Bad stuff that needs to go away, good stuff that needs time and patience to grow. We have wounds and gifts and needs and hopes, and all of these things can rule us if we don't know how to take charge. They run our lives, our decisions, even our tone of voice with the people we love. If you are controlled by wounds or unmet desires, then you may feel like you're stuck in a pinball machine, bouncing from one fear mechanism to another without any idea how to stop or slow down. In that out-of-control place, we don't know why we're doing what we're doing until after it's done.

But a confident girl doesn't have to live that way, especially if she has a place to put her stuff. She knows how to set aside the hard things and take control of her emotions. She knows how to save the good things so the waiting doesn't control her either. It doesn't mean she doesn't deal with these things; it just means she's in charge of how and when.

Sometimes an imaginary box can be exactly what you need to be in charge of your life again. You don't have to be stuck in the pinball machine anymore, dear girl. You can take charge of your life by choosing not to let it take charge of you. You can choose your very own box for your very own stuff and step forward with confidence.

## Stepping Forward

Maybe you have some stuff that needs a place to go. Perhaps you have an overwhelming sense of intense loneliness where intimacy used to be. Maybe you have fear that threatens to overtake you in the dark of the night. Maybe anxiety is ever close, begging for attention, and you need a metaphorical place to put it so it's out of your way. Or maybe you have some longings you've defined, some dreams delayed or hope deferred. It's very empowering when you have a box to put your stuff in, either to contain what has grown too big or to set something aside to think about later. It was a game changer for me, this realization that I am in control of invisible things like thoughts, longings, fears, and desires.

So create a box where you can put your stuff. But remember to make it big enough to hold it all, or Jana will make you start over and do it again. Choose wisely and be creative.

# CHAPTER 8

# Step Off the Merry-Go-Round

## The Confident Girl Feels How She Feels

*Ah! If you only knew the peace there is in an accepted sorrow.*

JEANNE-MARIE DE LA MOTTE-GUYON

**IT'S BEEN A WHILE NOW,** but in the first couple of years after Robb died, I landed in the emergency room because of panic attacks that wouldn't calm themselves. I couldn't slow down my breathing or quiet my adrenaline, and my family took me to the ER, where the doctors gave me enough sedatives to give a horse a nice nap.

One time, an ER nurse gave me great advice about my body having a physiological response to every single thought, subconscious or conscious. He said I can break the patterns and change my physiology. He said that when my thoughts start repeating like a broken record, it's time to scratch the record and begin again. Good advice. Excellent, actually. But it was somehow maddening, though I didn't know why.

When I took all of this to Jana, as we talked through the strategies the nurse recommended and the ones I have in place to combat anxiety, Jana simultaneously confirmed both what I was hoping and the reason I was frustrated by the nurse's advice: I was already doing all of those things. I had been learning and practicing these techniques for two years now. That's why it sounded familiar.

I remember racking my brain with frustration. *Why does this still happen? Why does anxiety simply put on a different mask and attack me from a new angle? Why can't I conquer it? Can I avoid this? Am I doing something wrong?* Here's what I learned: Sometimes the body simply needs to respond in the way it needs to respond. A person needs to laugh, as laughter releases endorphins with a compelling list of positive attributes. A person needs to cry in order to take the lid off the kettle, let out some steam, and release the pressure. If you train yourself not to cry—or worse, not to laugh—you're not doing yourself any favors.

Sure, we all need to learn how to manage the manifestation of these emotions so we don't laugh in a courtroom or cry at grand openings of supermarkets. (Although I have to say, I can get a little worked up over a new Super Target.) But sometimes you just need to laugh until you cry or cry until you laugh. The body needs to respond the way the body needs to respond.

There is a benefit to feeling how you feel when you feel it, to grieving when you need to. I discovered a profound grace in the first year after unfixable heartbreak: People expect grief to overwhelm. They expect the isolation, the empty mind, the wordlessness, the side effects, the absence of one's spirit.

But unfortunate is the one who cannot grieve in the window of grace. (*Unfortunate* is not a big enough word.) Doors fly open in the second year, no matter whether one hears the knock, no matter whether one turns the knob. Expectations rise with the sun. If a person has not done her crying, her aching, her bleeding—if she could not, for any reason at all—the grace does not last for always.

If her heart softens later, people may not understand what is happening inside her. I liken this to a child whose brain is not yet ready to read when phonics is part of the curriculum. If there's a sudden literary connection when he's eleven, instead of when he was seven, the work is remedial. His friends have moved on to chapter books. He has just begun to piece the letters together. They have begun to make sense to him. But he is behind.

My friend, if you missed your window, then you must simply create your window. Even if the world no longer expects you to feel, you must let yourself do the feeling. You must hold on to what is yours.

Let's talk about those two words: *Hold on.* I so want you to know what this means in the face of heartbreak, because we can't lose its worth to a meaningless cliché. "Hold on," I always said to my small children when I gave them my hand before we crossed the street. Climbers hold on to monkey bars so they won't fall. Skiers hold on to the waterskiing rope so that boat doesn't leave them behind. And it's a phrase we so often hand to the broken heart so close to giving up: "Hold on tight."

Here's what I know: You don't have to hold on tight when you are in charge. It's a reaction, a vulnerable choice, an act of anchoring. You don't hold on as a way of life; you hold on as a method of survival. You don't hold on forever—it's a passing posture on your way to rest. You hold on until the danger is gone, until your feet touch the ground, until you are safe again. So what does it mean to hold on when it's not a literal grip or grasp? Hold on . . . to what?

You hold on to whatever is keeping you from floating away. You find one thing that is solid, safe, and secure, and you don't let it out of your sight. Don't let it out of your grip. Hold on to the one thing you can find that is real and true. Your child. Your art. Your family. A playlist. A song. A phrase. A word. Hold on to that with both hands.

Stay here and hold on, believing that this is a passing posture you won't have to keep forever. It's just until the danger has passed, until your feet touch the ground, until you are safe again. Hold on, and believe in the balance of grace. Nothing stays terrible forever, and you need to do what you must do to weather the storm.

I mentioned that Jana and I have spent hundreds of hours together working through the dark and light of my story. I've often said that writing became my medication and that the books were my therapy, but it's important to add that this has been in addition to *real* medication and *real* therapy. And so, by the way, I'm still seeing Jana every week. Our conversations are less often about the widow in me anymore; now we talk more about this girl with misconceptions and boundaries and jacked-up perceptions from broken trust. It's not easy to be honest and true and vulnerable. There's a direct link between emotional energy and physical strength, and during a particularly grueling session, Jana watches me wilt before her. When my heart gets tired, I fade into the shell of myself. She patiently waits for me. I imagine that good therapists spend a lot of their time doing that: just waiting. She waits beside the cave and reminds me that I don't have to be in there all alone. She said recently, "Tricia, not talking about it doesn't mean it didn't happen. And talking about it doesn't make it any more true than it already was."

A confident girl lets herself grieve until she is finished. She feels how she feels simply because *it's how she feels*. It doesn't matter if it doesn't make sense to others; your feelings are theirs neither to explain nor to fix. Add to your dinner party: Find those people in your life who really do have patience and understanding and space for your grieving, and invite them to your table. Even if that makes it a table for just two. Step off the merry-go-round of the world's pace, and give yourself space to feel.

## Stepping Forward

Healing comes in telling the story a thousand times. For better and for worse, words give life and strength. It is a brave girl who will say them out loud. Tell your story in some way today, either to a friend over coffee, on the pages of a journal, in the post of a blog, or in art you create. If you're strong enough, do it again tomorrow. And next week. Let yourself feel; let yourself heal.

# CHAPTER 9

# Open Your Hands When a Gift Comes Along

## The Confident Girl Can Receive

*If you have been brutally broken, but still have the courage to be gentle to others then you deserve a love deeper than the ocean itself.*
NIKITA GILL

**THE SECOND LOVE STORY OF** my life began with a cup of coffee. After years of writing at the corner table of Starbucks, so prolifically and for so many hours straight that even my laptop smelled like coffee beans, I donned my own green apron and joined the baristas behind the counter. And on a Tuesday night, an incredibly handsome man came in for a latte that would change both of our lives forever.

"Welcome to Starbucks," I said. "What can I get started for you?"

He looked at my name tag and then opted for my nickname, as if we'd known each other for years. "Tricia . . . Trish, what are we going to put in this cup this evening?" He held up his shiny purple travel mug.

I began the litany of questions to help a guest make a decision. "Well, let's see. Did you want something hot or cold tonight?"

"Hot."

"And coffee or tea?"

He laughed, as if he'd ever be one to drink tea at Starbucks. "Let's go with coffee."

He told me that what he really wanted more than anything was some almond milk for his coffee. I'm sure glad Starbucks didn't offer almond milk back then, or I would have simply given him an almond milk latte and our conversation would have been over. Just another transaction and another satisfied customer on a forgettable Tuesday night. But instead, as I had been trained, I apologized that we didn't have exactly what he wanted, and I offered him every other kind of milk to make his drink complete. As it turned out, he was a former Starbucks partner, he knew there was no almond milk, and he was just giving me the runaround to see how I'd handle his antics. Ladies and gentlemen, I kept up. With playful banter and some witty flirting, it was the perfect meet-cute.

Peter says that he was intrigued from that very first conversation, and he wanted more. He began a lighthearted pursuit, coming back the next day to see if I was working. When I wasn't there, he came by the next day. And then the next. I came to expect him as a regular, to learn his coffee preferences, and I even started to get all fluttery when he was next in line. Peter just kept showing up for more coffee, and he talked me right out from behind the counter. He started coming at the end of my shift, sitting at the bar at the end of the counter, waiting for me to finish working so I might join him.

Before our first conversation over the counter, Peter had never heard my name. He hadn't read my writing, my blog, or any of my books, and I found that equal playing field very inviting and attractive. The nature of my writing and my work often invites people to learn a lot about me without the privilege of reciprocity, and I had often felt like first dates were always in the man's favor, as he knew way more about me than I did about him.

Instead, Peter and I began to learn each other's stories at the same time, and we studied each other as if there would be a test. I learned that he does impeccable accents and cartoon voices, from Kermit the Frog to Mrs. Doubtfire's perfect Scottish brogue. I learned that he's a recruiter, the CEO of his own company, and a networking genius. He's an old-fashioned guy, and he's unapologetically attached to his core values, his faith, his family, and especially his son and daughter. I met his two adult children, who are wonderful, smart, and hilariously funny. They quickly became my friends, and it took no time at all for me to enjoy them as their dad does.

I learned that Peter prioritizes things like making eye contact, writing thank-you notes, learning people's names, and creating significant conversations in the briefest moments. I discovered that he loves laughing, singing, and dancing; having honest conversations; and chasing after the Lord. He still had a slight advantage as he read my books, but each time we met, he brought his copies, flagged and noted, with questions and page numbers to reference. (Be still my heart.)

After many, many cups of coffee, he said, "You know, I know Starbucks is your safe place, and I'll keep coming here for as long as you want. But when you're ready to come out of your cocoon, I'd like to see if we can continue this conversation in other places." (Oh, I was definitely ready.) As it turns out, even a girl whose heart has been shattered can learn to trust again with enough time and courage. So he took me out for dinner, and he said, "Trish, let me ask you: Is this a date?"

He laid this question on the table, and I thought, *Wait, does he think I am going to be the one to define this relationship? No, sir, I did my time at a conservative Christian college. I know all about the DTR, thank you very much. Ain't no way I'm stepping into those waters without you leading the way.*

And so I answered, "You know, I think I'd like to respectfully defer to your definition of what this is."

He said, "Well, there's one thing we haven't talked about. I am, well"—and there was a long pause—"considerably older than you."

Eighteen years older, if we're counting. And it seemed like an important time to at least acknowledge the math. (Peter is a Boomer, and while I'm technically a Gen-Xer, I'm full of Millennial tendencies. At that point, it was only an issue of pop culture references. He would refer to something in the seventies or eighties, and I could always tell by the look on his face that the line he had just delivered would totally kill with a different audience. But fear not; it goes both ways. He rarely tracks my references to *Friends* or *Saved by the Bell*.)

He said, "I've done a little research, and I learned that there's a formula for such things. In order to acceptably date a younger woman, her age needs to be at least half his age, plus seven."

He watched me with a twinkle in his eye as I quickly solved for *x* in my mind. Whew! We were *just under the wire*!

And then Peter reached across the table and held his hand open to me. He said, "I can't imagine why you'd want to do life with me, but I want you to know, I'd like to give this a try. I love every single thing I know about you, and I only want more. If you'll have me, I'd like to woo this maiden, fight for her, and protect her. I'd like to steward what you've begun with your young men, and I'd like to invest in them. I'm not perfect, but I'm a really good tryer. If you'll let me, I'd like to give this a try."

He took my hand in his. He said, "What do you think? Would you let this old man have a shot at loving you?"

*Oh, for crying out loud.* They could have brought out a mop to clean me up off the floor. I said, "Yes, I believe I'd like to let you give that a try."

❧

My boys and I are a package. A buy-one-get-two-free deal. Together we had prayed so fervently for "the new dad." It was a tender process to walk them through, this journey of expectancy without expectation, of hope without promise. We knew we could ask forever and God might say no, but asking is part of believing in faith.

One year during the Advent season, a tender time for us because Robb had died two days before Christmas, I talked with the boys about something they had in common with the baby in the manger: Jesus grew up without his biological dad. Joseph married Mary, knowing she was pregnant with a child that was not his own. He knew that the marriage to her was a package deal, that the boy came with the girl. As a mom, I wondered whether he had to learn to love Jesus. I mean, I imagine Jesus was an easy kid, so maybe that part was easier. But Joseph wasn't his father. God was.

(And is.)

God planted in Joseph's heart a deep, bonding love to raise a child he had not conceived with his wife. This discovery deepened my prayer for "the new dad." Our Joseph, so to speak. I asked God to give this man, whose name and face I didn't know, a deep, bonding love to raise two boys who didn't start out as his own. I knew I would marry for nothing less.

One day soon after our first date, Peter came over for dinner with my boys and me. Over a pieced-together dinner of hot dogs and Doritos, Peter asked my sons to tell him the most important things about them. Tuck said he loves football and that his favorite parts of school are recess and lunch; Tyler said he was born with six fingers on his left hand and that he hates to be teased or tickled.

Peter said, "These are so important for me to know, you guys. See, the reason I'm asking is because I came into Starbucks a few weeks ago, and I met your mom. And I really like her. I just really *like-like* her. And so I'd like to spend some time with your family, and when I'm with someone, I like to know what matters to them, what they want me to know about them. So this is really good for me to know. I want to know about you."

Then he said, "What would you think if I spent some time with your mom? How would you feel about me dating her?"

Tuck's face lit up and he threw his arms up like he'd scored a touchdown. "Yes! Someone *finally wants to date my mom!*" (Nice, Tuck. Thanks, kiddo.)

Peter said, "Yes, someone sure does. I do."

Then Tuck quickly found his "take me seriously now" expression and said, "I have four requirements." He looked squarely at Peter.

"Yes, sir. Let's hear them," Peter said, picking up on the cues of this first man-to-man talk with my preadolescent son.

"First, you have to love God." Tuck counted on his fingers. "Second, you have to love my mom. Third, you have to love my brother and me, because we're a package deal. We come with her."

Peter nodded and solemnly took it all in. Then he said, "That's a great list, young man. I believe I can agree to all of those items. And what is the fourth?"

"You have to throw a football with me."

"Deal. I'm in for four out of four."

Satisfied, Tuck picked up his fork. "Okay. Then you can have her."

Peter said, "Men, we have something in common: I didn't have my dad when I was growing up either. My dad didn't die, but he just wasn't around in my home. So I grew up without him, and I know what it's like to just want to have your dad around. Tyler, I bet you'd really like to have your dad at your shows and musicals. And Tucker, I bet you'd really like to have your dad at your football games, just like the other guys on your team. Boys, I can't bring your dad back, and I'm so sorry you don't have him. But I'll tell you what. I'd like to be the man in the audience who's there just for you. What do you think about that?"

I stayed silent and stoic, but I was melting inside.

Tyler smiled. "I'm okay with that."

Tucker said, "I've waited five years for you, Peter. Finally you're here. Finally, someone can help me take care of my mom."

Peter said, "It's a big responsibility, Tuck. And I understand how you feel—I felt that way about my mom, like I had to look out for her all the time because nobody else was. So I promise you, from this day forward, I will never, ever hurt her. If you'll trust me, I'd like to be on your team. I'd like to take care of her, so you can work on just being ten years old."

"Okay," my tall son said. "Let's do that."

❧

One day we were riding in the car when eight-year-old Tyler spoke up from the backseat, his most consistent place for asking hard questions. I suspect there is something exponentially safer about hard topics when Mom's eyes are occupied with the road and other drivers.

"Mom, I just have one question."

"Ask me as many as you want, buddy."

"Will you still love my dad?"

"Oh, honey, yes. Forever, I will. He's the first man I ever loved, and he gave me you. I will love him always."

There was only silence.

I said, "Hey, buddy, think with me about when you read a book that you love, love, love. You love the characters, the story, the pictures—everything. And then you finish reading that book, and we put it on our bookshelf, and then we go to the library or the bookstore to choose another one, right?"

"Right." I was speaking the language of my bookworm.

"So, sometimes when you choose the next book, you discover this new book is your favorite too. You still love that book on the shelf, but that story is finished and you know how it ends. It's time to read a new one."

There was more silence.

"Honey, your dad is like our favorite book on the shelf. We can always love that story, and we can get it down to read it again and again. That was such a beautiful story, always one of our favorites. But that story is completed. We know how it ends, and we can start a new story now."

You see, I had begun to realize another very important truth for a confident girl: She must believe that her story isn't over. What feels like The End is perhaps only the last chapter in this season. The opposite of death is creating, and an end can be followed only by a beginning. Maybe there's another whole story to be written with your name in it. I needed to embrace for myself—and model for my sons—the confidence to believe our story wasn't over.

❧

And so it began. Peter wooed each of our hearts, all together and one at a time. He builds Legos with Tyler; he throws the football with Tucker. He listens to them and laughs with them. And God knows the honest truth: There's just so much to us. Legos on the floor. Seat belts. Spilled Gatorade. Unfinished homework. Incomplete grocery lists. Leftovers for dinner. Missing winter coats. Knots in shoelaces. Piles of laundry. Arguing. Whining. Football. Auditions. Clutter. Broken toys. Wayward Nerf bullets. Homework folders. Decisions. Grace. Love. Forgiveness. Laughter. Tears. Wounds. Worries. Healing. More football and more auditions. And it all requires heaps of endless patience.

In our earliest days together, I was embarrassed to let Peter see the magnitude of all of this. I asked him one frazzled evening, "Peter, why would you ever want to do this with us? We're so much. Too much."

He put his arms around me, resting his chin on my head. "Come here," he said. "Why would you say that?"

"Because we are one seriously hot mess. You could just quietly walk away before this gets further out of control, Peter. You could. You probably should."

He lifted my chin so my eyes met his. He said, "Well, that's what *you've* decided. Do I get a vote?" (Sometimes there comes a moment of clarity when I realize that what sounds like an exit strategy is really just my own pride and fear getting in the way.)

I leaned into him with my ear against his chest, listening to his solid heartbeat. "Yes, you get a vote."

He wouldn't let me break eye contact. He brought my eyes back to his. "Tricia, I want to do this. All I can tell you is that this isn't an effort for me. It's where I want to be. Any who have told you that you're too much have only been weak men who don't know how to lead and love well. As long as I get a vote, I'm in. You're not too much for me."

I had carried this great heaviness for so long—so very, very long—and I could sense a finish line. Aside from the absolutely overwhelming, disorienting, feet-knocked-out-from-under-me, oh-my-great-day feelings of falling in love, the greatest emotions I felt in that season were a deep and distracting fear as well as a sense of such consuming almost-rest.

I was almost to a place where I could set it down. But instead of setting it down with a great sense of relief, I found my arms trembling with fear, my eyes welling with tears, and my spirit saying, "Can I? Can I set this down? Can I stop carrying? Is it okay?"

The thing is, deciding to receive something good is a little bit terrifying—and sometimes a lot bit. For me, this good thing was the love of a good man, and falling in love is very undoing. Falling in love after knowing the very color of death in the eyes you have trusted is every kind of terrifying. There was so much fear in the way. Only a widow truly knows how much she stands to lose. When your greatest joy has slipped through your fingers, it's unspeakably difficult to open your hands again to hold something new. I learned firsthand that this kind of receiving is a conscious choice, a decision.

I wanted to trust the man in front of me, and I wanted to trust the Giver of this good and perfect gift. I wanted to believe the sun could shine in our home again. I so badly wanted to be a confident girl who could believe that God had heard our prayers all along, that he truly had seen every tear my children had cried, that he is the father to the fatherless, the defender of the widow, and that he could answer us with *yes*.

In the first year after Robb died, that very Starbucks was my safest place. It was my only place. I went there every morning, and I took my journal and my Bible, and I copied the Psalms when I didn't know how to talk to God. When I couldn't pray, I let the psalmists pray for me. In that space, I found courage and honesty and a voice . . . and my confidence to continue on in this life I felt left alone to live. So wouldn't it be just like the kindness and playful genius of him, the God who sent a newborn king into an unsuspecting world, to quietly send my new husband into my life through the very Starbucks that had been my sanctuary, the place where God had been restoring me all along?

If I could believe that was true, then I wanted to accept his gift with confidence and open hands.

That's when I began to learn that sometimes confidence

is a journey of one day at a time. Falling in love is a rushing waterfall; trust is a fortress built brick by brick. It's true in my relationship with God; it's true in a marriage; it's true for anyone who stands on the brink of letting someone in. And so, one day at a time—and one conversation at a time—I began to trust God that Peter could hold my pieces. And I started to let Peter lift the world off my shoulders.

Several months after that Tuesday night when I first poured coffee into Peter's empty cup, sans almond milk, he came in yet again, this time on a Friday morning. I spotted him when he got in line for a cup of coffee. He seemed so centered, so grounded, so peaceful. He stepped up to the counter, next in line. And this sly, silver fox said to me, so evenly and with so much intention, "Trish, I came in here a few months ago, and I asked you to fill up my coffee cup. Today I would like to ask you for something more."

And then his eyes got shiny with tears and his mouth made an almost-frown that means he's about to cry. And then, he got down on one knee, he pulled a diamond ring out of his pocket, and he held it out to me across the counter. And everything in the world disappeared except this man before me, on one knee.

"Trish," he said, "will you be my wife?"

For the rest of my life I'll be embarrassed to say what happened next, that for just a moment, a too-long moment, I was so overcome that I forgot to answer him. I left the poor man kneeling on the floor in a crowded coffee shop, while he waited for me to find breath and words. The poor guy just waited.

I had no words. None.

But then I said yes. Because of course I said yes. A million times yes. For the rest of my life, yes.

I ran from behind the counter, and I literally leapt into his arms. He swept me up into his arms and he kissed me, and the morning coffee crowd erupted with cheers and applause. It was only then that I realized there was anyone else in the room or in the world. For that moment, everything else had fallen away; there was only Peter and a diamond ring and the look on his face that I want to remember for all of my days.

We were married three months later in my backyard. It was a perfect day and a glorious beginning with a celebration that put all the grieving to rest. We are in the throes of building a life together: this man and me, our four children, our three dogs, our pillow conversations, and our morning cups of coffee.

Have you heard of Starbucks' new rewards program? If you buy enough cups of coffee, you get a wife.

PETER

*P.S. Remember that invisible box I mentioned in chapter 7? The white one with the red satin ribbon? Peter loved it. (And everything in it.)*

# Stepping Forward

As Peter and I began to fall in love, just past the sparklers of infatuation but before the questions of commitment, I remember sitting with a friend and holding my hands in balance, weighing the life I knew against the realm of possibilities with someone new. She put her hands in mine, canceling the balancing and the weighing of the pros and cons. She said, "Tricia, now is the time to be brave. Just take another step in his direction. It's time to stop the search and take a risk."

I had grown so accustomed to waiting that I could have let it become a habit. I could have cautioned my way into a long life of loneliness, but life is too short to be too careful. Set your guardrails and guidelines, and of course, be wise. But when you lay before God the desires of your heart, be ready to move forward when his answer is *yes*.

Think of the things you're waiting for, hoping for, asking for. I can promise you this: God sees you, hears you, and is for you. He's working on something that may be silently growing in ways you can't see. But very often, God's blessings look different than we expect, and we can miss the gift if it's wrapped in a different package.

Ask him for eyes to see what he has given you, and for open hands to receive what is next. Ask God to give you courage to wait during the season of growing, and confidence to step forward into a season of plenty.

# CHAPTER 10

# Share Your Kindness

*The Confident Girl Sprinkles Kindness Like Confetti*

*I discovered I always have choices and sometimes it's only a choice of attitude.*
JUDITH M. KNOWLTON

**REMEMBER THAT LITTLE** girl in her Betsy Ross costume? Let's go back to that girl. Because the story isn't over.

I came home with all of the Betsy Ross costuming and paraphernalia, and I shoved it all into a corner of my closet. The next day, when I was supposed to wear it, I couldn't bring myself to put it back on. I didn't want to try again. Could you blame me? It was all too much. I was so homesick for my old school. I begged my parents to withdraw me from this new place. I wanted to go back to the teachers, the hallways, the playground, the very everythings I remembered in the safe nest of the school we had left behind. I even missed the smell of the hand soap in the bathroom. I started my campaign to abort this stupid mission and go back to the land from whence I had come.

"She hates me, Mom. She hates me."

"Tricia, now let's think about this. Teachers don't hate their students. She's just not as kind as the other teachers you have had. I promise, she doesn't hate you."

"I think she does, though."

"She doesn't hate you."

"Then she really, really, really, *really* doesn't like me. At all."

I begged and pleaded to go back to my old school, but sadly, it was all to no avail. There is a reason little people are born to big people, and the decision wasn't mine to make. My fate was sealed in my new school, and together we would have to find a way to make this work.

My mom has always had a way to get her kids on board with her great ideas, and she presented a plan that would call for some seriously clever thinking. She said, "Well, we're going to play a little game, you and me. Every day before you get on the school bus, we will think of something nice you can say to Mrs. Wretched when you see her. And every single time she looks at you, smile at her."

"Mom, she doesn't smile. Not at all."

"And that's a terrible way for her to go through life, but she doesn't have to smile for our game to work. The only one who has to smile is you. Because here's the truth: It's pretty easy to like someone who smiles first. With all your smiles and kind words, we'll trick her into liking you."

I was skeptical, but I didn't have any better ideas. So we set the plan in motion. *Operation: Smile First.*

I remember standing inside the front door, watching

for the headlights of the bus through the line of pine trees. I breathed my hot air onto the window, drawing hearts in the fog I'd just made with my own steam, and I practiced the things I would say to Mrs. Wretched. I practiced so that I could learn the sound of my own voice, just in case it failed me in the moment when I needed it to sound kind and confident. *Your hair looks nice today, Mrs. Wretched. That's a pretty blouse you're wearing, Mrs. Wretched. I like your handwriting on the board, Mrs. Wretched.* Every morning, I told her my practiced compliment. And she never, ever said anything in return. She barely grunted any recognition of my voice at all.

A few weeks into the school year, my parents attended an open house at the school. Finally in a setting with adults only, my parents could approach her as a peer. My mom said, "Tricia seems to think you don't like her."

With folded arms and zero sense of irony, she told my parents, "Oh, I like all of my students. I just don't smile very often. When I smile, they know they've done something truly outstanding."

Okay, first of all, this: Teachers should smile. If you hoard your smiles for some unknown reason, then don't go into a profession that thrives on them. Actually, I'm not sure what job I should recommend to you, since a smile is the most basic gift you can give another human being. Deep down inside, every one of us wants to be liked. If you simply show people that you like them, they will want to like you right back. It's pretty foolproof advice. But for the sake of humanity, be a person who smiles. This is especially true if you're going to teach children who are prone to letting your temperament set their emotional barometer.

My mom was the very picture of diplomacy because, well, she just always is. But she was so stunned by Mrs. Wretched's explanation that she didn't have a response at all. That's when she knew I had been right all along. In convincing me that Mrs. Wretched didn't hate me, she was only off by a single phrase: Mrs. Wretched didn't hate me; she hated children in general.

Now that I'm a mother too, my mom has said that she can't recall why on earth she didn't at least speak with school administration and have me placed in a different fourth-grade class—since there were, after all, eight fourth-grade teachers to choose from. But it was all new territory for her, too. She didn't know the power of her voice in the public school system, she didn't know how many chips she had to play, and school culture "back then" wasn't as it is today, where parents can make phone calls to demand changes great and small to make things go the way they want them to go. When she realized how right I was, all she could do—or all she thought she could do—was intensify her coaching and encourage me to smile and say something nice every day. So she set about it.

What I couldn't have known at the time was that this day-after-day practice of *Operation: Smile First* was instilling in me the root of determined confidence. I decided what I would do, how I would conduct myself, and even the joy I would bring to that classroom, despite Mrs. Wretched's suffocating presence. As it turns out, that's one of the foundational pieces of a confident life: being who you will be, offering your own beauty into the world, and believing there is a place for it in the darkness.

I stayed in Mrs. Wretched's class for one very, very long year. There was no way to measure the success of *Operation: Smile First* until months later—on the *very last day of the school year*—when my mom came to school to see me in the spelling bee. (I didn't win. I lost on the word *missile*, which I very unfortunately spelled *m-i-s-t-l-e*. In my defense, I was thinking of *mistletoe*. I know I'm digressing from the point at hand, but if you ask anyone who's ever lost a spelling bee, we can't talk about spelling bees without recalling the word we will never misspell again. For the rest of our lives, spellers care deeply about the word we got wrong. Forgive us the neurosis; we can't help ourselves.)

In the little reception for the spellers, over crunchy cookies and Dixie cups of pink lemonade, Mrs. Wretched came to my mom. She said, "Tricia is the nicest little girl, and I've so enjoyed having her in class. She always has such a sweet smile on her face, and she always has something nice to say."

Well, glory be. It. Had. *Worked.*

All of those days, stacked right on top of one another for months upon months, all of them culminated in one moment when my mom's eyes met mine on that very last day before summer, when I finally learned that Mrs. Wretched had noticed. Somewhere along the way, in the silence of her own heart that she certainly never confirmed aloud, Mrs. Wretched had decided to like me.

My mom cries all over again every time she thinks of her eyes catching mine in that moment. There was something so important about the fact that we had determined—even if Mrs. Wretched never said a word, even if she was mean all year long—that I could still choose to be who I wanted to be, regardless of what she thought. And in a moment that cemented who I would forever become, I learned that *it had worked*.

Shakti Gawain says, "An affirmation is a strong, positive statement that something is *already* so."[1] When you affirm yourself or someone else, you're declaring that you see something positive in him or her—something positive in yourself. In *Operation: Smile First*, I learned this practice of affirmation, of giving a gift with my words, and it has become a language of mine, a way of loving other people. I am generous with affirmation and encouragement, and here's what I've found: People like you when they believe you like them. Everyone loves to be seen and known. When they feel that *you* have seen them and known them, then they love you. And when people love you, you feel more confident. That's the bottom line of the whole thing, the basis for the whole book: Be nice to people, and your confidence will be contagious. (You can stop reading now if you want. I hope you continue to stick with me, though. If only for the stories and the coffee stains.)

꧁

There's one more piece of this kindness thing that we need to talk about, and Gideon is going to help us get there. Gideon is one of my heroes in the Bible. I like him because he and I have a lot of the same tendencies: He's one of the most fearful and doubtful individuals in the Bible. When God came to tell Gideon that God had chosen him to lead his people to freedom, God found Gideon threshing wheat in hiding, a task that was normally done in public outside the city. But Gideon was afraid of the Midianite army, so he hid and did his work in silence and solitude. The story says the angel of the Lord appeared and said, "The LORD is with you, mighty warrior."

Gideon responds as I have sometimes: "If the LORD is with us, why has all this happened to us?"[2] His response is so similar to what I've occasionally wondered: *Wouldn't God deliver me from this, if he's on my side?*

Oh, Gideon, how I love you. How I get you.

But God faces him directly and calls him to action. He says to Gideon, "Go in the strength you have."[3]

Once again, and also in a move I understand, Gideon responds out of insecurity. He says, "How? . . . My clan is the weakest in Manasseh, and I am the least in my family."[4] In other words, Gideon responds to God with "the tape." Everyone has one. Everyone has the mental recording of someone else's words, someone who made us obviously aware of how small, how unprepared, how unextraordinary we are.

Can't you just picture it? Maybe little boy Gideon was at the dinner table with his family, and he finally decided he'd had enough of some of his boyhood frustrations. And in his indignation (which is not hard for me to picture since I'm raising one child in particular who is especially prone to indignation), maybe he raised his little fist in the air to say, "That is *it*! I have had *enough*!"

And maybe his family smiled, his mom patted him on his little noggin, and his dad said, "Oh, Gideon, it's so cute when you're so mad. But don't you know that you're the youngest member of the smallest family in the weakest tribe of Manasseh? What on earth could you do to make a change around here?"

And just like that, a mental tape recording falls into place. We know because Gideon was quick with his answer to God: "But I'm in the smallest family in the weakest tribe." He'd said that before.

But God stopped the tape and called Gideon to see him as God saw him: as a *mighty warrior*. He called Gideon to him, and he said, "Go in the strength you have." He didn't say, "Go in the strength you will eventually have" or "Go in the strength you will have after you finish reading this book" or "Go in the strength you will have when you lose ten pounds" or even "Go in the strength you will have when you know more about me." No, he commissioned him in the strength Gideon already had.

So here's the final important thing about kindness: It's a battle for all of us mighty warriors. There are so many of you with a toxic sound-bite playing on repeat. Every time God has a call for you, you play that sound-bite again, and say you're not in the right spot, you're not the right gender, you don't have the right skills. I'm with you, sisters. But God is asking us to stop the tape. Stop listening to those words, and instead replace them with who God says you are. The person you spend the most time with is you, so be careful and intentional about how you speak to yourself. Kind words go a long, long way, just as I learned in Mrs. Wretched's classroom. And sometimes you need to use them with yourself, especially when you have a Gideon-like loop playing on repeat.

## Stepping Forward

Think about the confidence thief you identified all the way back in chapter 1, and recall the words they said to you or even just the seed they planted in your mind about yourself. Now write an affirmation to yourself, about yourself, that stands in direct opposition to what that person made you believe. Our minds cannot work with a vacuum; they fill up every available space with whatever thoughts are available. If we are going to rid ourselves of painful words that have grown deep roots, they have to be replaced with something. That's what God did when he said to Gideon: "I am with you. And you are a mighty warrior." Gideon needed a new tape. Maybe you do too.

One powerful thing you can do is to speak positive affirmations based on the truths of the Bible. I have a card system that I carry around with me in my computer bag. It's a ziplock bag filled with three-by-five cards, and on each one I've written a truth from Scripture. I've found that I don't always have time to look up those verses when I need them, and even the best memorization techniques fail sometimes. But I've begun keeping a card or two in the drawer by my bed, in the console of my car, or as the bookmark in the novel I'm currently plowing through. As I keep the words handy, reading them when I see them, they begin to soak into the pockets of my spirit and the corners of my mind.

Find Scripture that you identify with, and then personalize it in a way to speak truth into your own life. If you can adapt Scripture to speak directly into your confidence wounds, then it's a double win. Pick one of the Scripture affirmations you identify with. Write it ten times. As you read these to yourself, you are literally renewing your mind, and that is the path to emotional freedom and confidence. Post these affirmations on your bathroom mirror, on the steering wheel of your car, as a scrolling message on your iPad, or on your refrigerator. The refrigerator is my favorite, because the whole family gets to enjoy the truth. And when your kids see these words, they'll begin to believe it's true of their mom—and their God. Because it is.

Start your own card system. Give it a try. Here are some examples to begin your collection.

- I am strong and courageous, for the Lord my God is with me wherever I go.[5]

- I am valuable and lovable and beautiful, for I am fearfully and wonderfully made.[6]

- Because I seek the Lord with all my heart, I lack no good thing.[7]

- I am worthy of living an abundant life—as Jesus intended.[8]

- My negative feelings do not come from God, and I don't need to listen to them.[9]

- I have strength and peace, and these come from the Lord.[10]

- I am a confident woman, and there is a place for me in the life I have.[11]

- My life brings honor to God.[12]

- I have complete confidence, O God. I will sing and praise you.[13]

# CHAPTER 11

# Carry a Sharpie in Your Pocket

## The Confident Girl Sets Boundaries

*Daring to set boundaries is about having the courage to love ourselves, even when we risk disappointing others.*

BRENÉ BROWN

**MY BROTHER IS** an actor at Walt Disney World, which means I have bonus reasons to claim it as one of my favorite places in the world. We love to visit him and all his personal friends— Mickey, Minnie, Woody, Buzz, and all the princesses. You might think the whole scene loses its magic when you know somebody on the inside, but that's not been the case for us. Everything—and most especially my brother—is more magical. We're all pretty enchanted by him, this guy who walks on a cloud of pixie dust in our minds. We arrive at the parks, and we turn off our decision-making abilities. He becomes our tour guide, taking us from front-row seats at this parade to VIP seating for that show, often including backstage passes and one-on-one meet and greets. There's nothing like a visit to Disney World if Rob is your brother, and since I'm his only sibling, I claim first rights to this incentive package—after only my parents, the very first keepers of the dream.

On one visit, Rob was telling us about "face characters"— the actors who are hired because they naturally look like the actual characters. As it turns out, there are a few cast members hired from their day jobs as cashiers or servers because the head of casting encountered them and said something like "My, you have the perfect facial structure to play Gaston" or "You have the doe-like eyes of Jasmine." I imagine this to be the best day-maker ever, to have someone happen into my day and tell me that I'm made of Disneyesque perfection.

Caught in my own daydream, I asked him who he thought I would be, hoping he would say Cinderella or Ariel or Belle—you know, those lovely princess-like creatures who undoubtedly resemble his lovely sister. (I was hopeful.) But no, instead he stated with pure confidence, "Oh, you would be Cruella de Vil."

Of course. I left that one wide open for him.

I should have seen it coming, because first a brother, always a brother. It would have been a rupture of the Bro Code if he hadn't walked right through that open door.

Anyway, all of that to say, we love Disney World. Even Cruella.

On a recent trip to Orlando, we were right in the middle of a great day at Disney's Hollywood Studios, one of my favorite parks. Tower of Terror. The Indiana Jones Epic Stunt Spectacular. Rock 'n' Roller Coaster. Movie sets and adventure rides and cast members and guest stars. We were up to our Mickey Mouse ears in parades and pixie dust in the park that happens to be my most favoritest place in the most magical place on earth. I was having a wonderful day with my crowd when quite suddenly and unexpectedly, it was all too much for me. It was too loud and too hot and too exhausting and too everything. I have the heart of an extrovert adventurer, but the rest of me carries characteristics of an agoraphobic introvert. There are limits to the big, loud fun I can have. I am not who I once was, and that's just how it is—perhaps how it will always be. Against my every instinct, I had to excuse myself and take a bus back to the hotel. I started the day with my family, and I intended to maintain the day with them, but sometimes a boundary hits and anxiety triggers, and I can't explain it or talk myself out of it. I simply know that I cannot stay involved for one more minute.

In deciding to leave, I knew I would miss some magical moments in the lives of my children. I knew I would have to settle for secondhand accounts later. I risked seeming ungrateful to my brother and sister-in-law, who make such magical moments possible at all. I knew I was missing out, even as I stepped away from all of the once-in-a-lifetime greatness. But I also knew, even as I stepped away, that I was taking care of my own needs, not just selfish wants. I was putting on my own proverbial oxygen mask first. I could save and restore the energy I had in order to be the mom my children would still need me to be later, when the parades turned to memories and the fireworks turned to smoke. It's never an easy decision, and in such moments of turmoil, I argue with myself long before I decide and long after I've decided. Ultimately, I look at the cards in my hands, and I make the best bet with what I've been dealt. Back to the hotel I went.

Boundaries don't come naturally to me. Jana and I have worked on this protocol for months. (Well, years.) I have a deep and wide capacity to love and feel deeply. I fill my moments with experiences, my life with goals, and my heart with people. Sometimes this is a wonderful thing, and sometimes I start to topple over with all that I'm carrying. I am learning that sometimes one has to step away from the awesome. Sometimes you have to run the risk of disappointing the crowd and missing out on the memory, because sometimes you have to take care of you, even if it doesn't make sense to anybody else. Sometimes it may not even make sense to you, either.

I chose the example from a day at Disney World because it's a relatively easy one—my family was with me to stand in full support and even to keep the magic alive for my children while I slipped back to the hotel to be quiet for a little while. They didn't disagree with my decision—they supported me while I argued with myself. That is often how it goes: Sometimes my worst challenges in setting boundaries are the arguments with myself.

❧

For a moment, picture the beautiful thick line of a Sharpie.

(I think it's entirely possible that on the eighth day, God

created Sharpies. I could write such a sonnet about these markers, their many colors and widths, the options and possibilities hiding inside a brand-new package. Oh, Sharpies, how I love you. You are my favorite accessory.)

(No, wait. Bracelets are my favorite accessory.)

(I may have an accessories problem. But there are worse vices to have. Whatever. I practice self-control in other ways.)

A Sharpie is good for so many things: doodling, drawing lovely margins, drawing lovely doodles *in* the margins. I have a friend who carries a Sharpie in her pocket to correct mistakes on public signage. Apostrophes for plural nouns are her archnemesis, and she will correct them wherever they show up. This particular issue is especially present at sidewalk markets. Farmers love to offer lots of *banana's* and *asparaguses'*.) She also blatantly fixes bathroom signs that say "employees must wash their hands before returning to work." She changes *employees* to *everyone*, and she changes *work* to *life*. I think we can all agree that she's right about this, even though she might be taking on a little too much with all the crossing out of signs that aren't hers.

Anyway, the best thing about Sharpies is the rich, thick lines you can make with a rich, thick Sharpie. They frame whatever you're doing, put a limit to where your eyes are supposed to go on that page. Sharpies are made for boundaries. A mentor in my life pats me on the back every time she sees me set boundaries with my children, my time, or toxic people in my life. She'll quietly affirm, "Good job, Trish. You get out that Sharpie, and you draw a real thick line. Well done." That's what a confident girl does: She sets boundaries. So get out your Sharpies, girls. Let's create a few boundaries.

Boundaries are boundaries, and the same rules apply whether you're setting them with children, schedules, or relationships. I've spent a lot of years learning about boundaries, so here are a few dozen therapy hours boiled down into a paragraph: Clearly identify your boundary, and understand why you need it. Be straightforward about your boundary, but don't apologize or give long explanations. "All you need to say is simply 'Yes' or 'No.'"[1] Remember that a boundary isn't about telling someone else what to do; it's about deciding what *you* will do—so no need to deal with self-made drama, tears, or arguments. Start with tighter boundaries, and then loosen up if it's appropriate (but know that you never have to change your mind). Learn the art of saying no: You don't have to lie, apologize, or overexplain. Just decline. Finally and always, trust your intuition. If it doesn't feel right, it's not right.

Boundaries with your time are tricky. I have this important quote doodled in some important places in my life: *No for Now Isn't No Forever.* I remind myself that saying no to myself when I want to say yes holds the implicit promise that maybe I can say yes later.

An example in my life is my brief foray into grad school. I have always wanted to go to grad school, and a few years ago, I took my first courses toward a Master of Fine Arts degree. But it didn't take me long to realize schedules, extensive study, and assignment deadlines were not a good fit for this season of my life. I gathered myself one day and walked into Jana's office with my tentatively worded statement: "I withdrew from grad school, Jana."

"Oh, did you?" She jotted this on her notebook, undoubtedly adding it to her list of baby steps I've taken.

"Yes. I don't need that right now. I mean, you're encouraging me to eliminate things that are unnecessary, anything that can go. Grad school? That's not something I need to do right now."

She smiled her knowing smile. "Well, you needed to come to that conclusion on your own."

"I did. I might go back someday. Or I might not. I don't really know. But I'm not finishing it now. And this idea of taking time to rest? Thinking of other things and not pushing myself quite so hard? It's pretty great."

"Yeah, that's called balance, by the way."

*No for Now Isn't No Forever.* Be brave enough to say no for now, knowing that maybe you can say yes later when the timing, margins, and self-care are right. Boundaries are a safe place to start to take care of yourself, your strength, your joy, and your dignity. They are not about right and wrong, and your own boundaries might look very different from someone else's. I've become an expert in setting my own boundaries, and I've found it beautifully energizing to set them. Boundaries don't mean I'm selfish or entitled; they mean that I know myself and what I need.

My friend Rebecca's greatest challenge is the capacity of her own heart. She is deeply gifted with compassion, mercy, and empathy, and she is undeniably compelled to bring people under her wing. Widows come to her for comfort and for school supplies for their children. She becomes a stand-in grandma for children who are lonely. Addicts come to stay in her home until they get back on their feet. She loves like nobody I know, and I can attest to the healing properties in her homemade chicken noodle soup. The woman has magic in her soul.

But she's *tired.* She's *really very, very tired.* She wears her heart on the outside, as if she has no skin. Did you ever fall off your bike as a kid, skinning your knee or elbow with road rash? There's no pain like road rash, when even the gentle wind hurts like mad. This reminds me of how Rebecca receives the happenings of a hurting world. Every need falls on her and sticks. Everything hurts.

She told me recently about hosting a friend and the friend's son for lunch. The boy is a little professor, bright and forever inquisitive. He's the kind who looks up definitions to every new word he hears, the kind of child who could construct intergalactic space cities created to scale from paper clips and tinfoil. His father had died recently, his mother was healing from an endlessly broken heart, and the little boy found solace in the sanctuary of Rebecca's backyard. He was fascinated by the flowers in her garden, and when he found her porch swing, he rocked himself back and forth until tears streamed down his face. Rebecca told me how it so blessed her to be a blessing to this family, and then she said, "But I don't know how I can continue to give them everything they need."

Ah, there it is, the compulsion among the boundaryless: *How can I give everyone everything they need?* But just because there's a need doesn't mean you are the answer.

I am not nearly so gifted with compassion and empathy, and on my lesser days I may seem kind of heartless next to Rebecca's endless giving. I have another friend who laughingly boasts that one of his spiritual gifts is insensitivity. He has no problem saying the hard thing to solve the problem, even if it's hard to hear. The world needs that kind of giftedness, too. There's a spectrum for bandwidth and compassion, and perhaps we can each balance one another with our boundaries.

I've learned how to separate myself from every need around me, and I gave Rebecca my dose of perspective: "What if your backyard sanctuary was a onetime gift? Maybe the gift of that day exists on its own, and maybe it doesn't mean you have to scoop up the family and carry them in your backpack now, inviting them over every Tuesday for afternoon porch-swing therapy."

She reached across the table and grabbed my hand with relief. "Thank you for saying that. Thank you. Because I just don't think I can carry one more thing." Backpacks get heavy. Sometimes you have to empty them to see what all you're carrying. You have to spread it all out on the kitchen table and take inventory. Then decide what you'll put back in the bag, what you really need to carry.

I wanted Rebecca to see that not every gift comes with a recurring membership, like a magazine subscription. Some gifts are more like an ice cream cone. When a child finishes an ice cream cone, it's not your job to hurry and scoop them another one to make the gift keep giving. Just let it be what it was: a gift that stands alone.

I'm not saying that Rebecca's friend is one of these, but I've known people who really want me to make their problem *my problem*. Those who are emotionally unhealthy will let you take on way more responsibility than should ever be yours. I heard this analogy somewhere about what this is like: Imagine you're walking along one day, minding your own business on a sunny day. You cross a bridge over a river, and a person approaches you. Kindly and gently, they say, "Would you hold this rope for me?"

Being the kind, gentle person you are, you assess the situation and see no harm in saying yes. Sure, you can do this person the quick favor of holding the rope. They hand you the rope, and then the person proceeds to tie the other end of the rope around their waist and jump off the bridge. They leave you holding not only the rope but a greater dilemma: If you let go of the rope, that person will crash to the ground.

Have you ever felt that way? Have you ever felt like you simply said yes to something small, and now the problem has been transferred and you're left holding the rope? I have. And it's a horrible place to stand. If you're not careful, you can feel hopelessly in charge of somebody else's mess.

Boundaries give you the ability to pull the cell phone from your pocket, call 911, hand the rope to the professionals when they arrive, and then quietly leave the scene. Boundaries give you the option to say, "This problem is bigger than me, and I can't fix this." Boundaries give you the clarity to know you can set something down carefully and walk away; if it crashes, it's not because you dropped it. Boundaries give you the courage to say, "My job here is done."

The tricky thing is this: It's not only the draining relationships that get us mixed up. The especially unhealthy ones, the ones that have hurt us deeply, are just as complicated. Somehow, a lot of us "nice Christian girls" have gotten a confusing list of expectations when it comes to relational boundaries. We somehow think that forgiveness means reconciliation and a restoration of the old ways of doing things. My friends, it's just not true. It is entirely possible and completely okay to forgive someone and yet still not want to spend time with him or her. Some friendships may be so damaged by sin and hurt that they cannot be restored this side of heaven. Pay attention when people react with anger or hostility to your boundaries. Sometimes the end of someone else's respect for you can become the beginning of your respect for yourself. Anyone who truly wants to be in your life for the right reasons will respect your boundaries.

Boundaries with people are the hardest boundaries to set, and you may not even know yet if you have a problem setting them. Here are a few signs that perhaps the boundaries in your life are blurry:

- **Your relationships are difficult or overly dramatic.** When you struggle to set boundaries, you send a signal to other people that you cannot take care of yourself. This leaves you susceptible to relationships with people who want to control you, and control is only ever dramatic and manipulative. Healthy relationships exist between people who have a healthy and mutual give-and-take in their friendship.

- **You find it difficult to make decisions.** When you don't have healthy boundaries in place, you spend a lot of time doing what other people want you to do. You don't know what you want or don't want, and you might not have a strong sense of who you are, what you like, and what matters most to you.

- **You *really, really, really hate* to let other people down.** We all like to maintain a positive scorecard in our relationships, so it's nice when the people in your life are happy. But people without boundaries worry excessively about letting other people down, so they hate to say no. If you've ever been called a "people pleaser," you might need to set some boundaries in your life.

- **You often feel guilt, fear, or anxiety.** People with boundary issues feel responsible if others are unhappy, and they feel guilty for small and insignificant things. They apologize often for things far beyond their control, and they carry a self-imposed responsibility for the world's happiness.

- **You feel inexplicably tired for no reason.** Always doing what other people want you to do leaves little time for you to take care of yourself and your own needs. This pattern is flat-out exhausting.

The confident girl loves herself enough to set boundaries. Your time and energy belong to you first, so you get to decide how to use them. You teach people how to treat you by deciding what you will and won't accept. At first you will probably feel selfish, guilty, or embarrassed for setting a boundary. Do it anyway. Get out your Sharpie and draw a real thick line. (The color choice, of course, is up to you. But I'd highly recommend green. Or blue. Or red. Or a nice four-pack.)

## Stepping Forward

Make a list of ten things you love doing with your time. Can you identify these quickly? It means you know yourself well.

Make a list of ten things you hate doing. What classes, hobbies, or pastimes drain your energy more than they fill it—but you participate because your friends expect you to? Pay attention to what matters to you, and don't let anyone coerce you into doing something you don't want to do.

Do you say yes to every seemingly worthwhile request, though you know you don't have the time or energy to add it to your calendar? Think on this—anything from bringing a meal to a sick friend, to babysitting for friends because their sitter canceled, to going to the Christmas party that you stopped enjoying a few years ago and that now is just an annual holiday obligation. What would you like to say no to? What would take a load off your shoulders if you could just set the boundary? Say no to something today, and rest in the confidence that this one word is a complete sentence. When you say no to something good, you can say yes to something better.

Read *Boundaries* by Henry Cloud and John Townsend. It will change your life and set you free in all the best ways.

# CHAPTER 12

# Never Drop the Same Plate Twice in a Row

## The Confident Girl Is a Confident Mom

*It's impossible to enjoy anything when you're afraid of failing at it. But once you know with all your heart that you really do have what it takes, being a mom can be a lot more fun.*

JOYCE MEYER, *THE CONFIDENT MOM*

**TUCKER WAS A FEW WEEKS OLD,** and it was my first night back at my part-time job as a writing teacher. I'm pretty sure I was teetering under the weight of everything I carried into my parents' house: the car seat, the diaper bag, bottles, milk, Binkies, blankets, burp cloths, a page of typed instructions, and finally, my newborn baby boy. Aside from my full hands, I carried a heart heavy with heaps of anxieties as a new mom. I placed everything in my mom's hands and in her care, and as I snuggled Tucker and kissed his face one more time, I said, "Mom, can you please hold him a lot tonight? I think I didn't hold him enough today."

First of all, let's address how gracious she was to entertain my anxieties about leaving my son in her care, after she had in fact raised me with few to no major errors in childcare decisions. She let me rattle off my list of instructions, acting and listening as though she were a novice at all things babycare, just recently trained and certified by the Red Cross.

She then gave me this gift that I have carried with me every day since. As I asked her to fill in the gaps I had left by not holding him all day long, she hugged me and said with a gentle smile, "Trish, you can feel guilty about that if you *want* to, but honestly, there will be so many real things for you to feel guilty about as a mother. I wouldn't waste my energy on that if I were you."

Somehow, she both acknowledged and dismissed my conviction in one fell swoop. And she was so right! I couldn't have imagined then how many times I would lie awake and wish I could do parts of the day over again—this time with patience and a more gentle voice. Sometimes I wish I could pick and choose which parts of my parenting my children will remember and which ones will be cast aside as deleted scenes. I contend that behind every great kid is a mom who's pretty sure she's screwing it up. The truth is that if you're worried about screwing up your child, then you're already a better mom than you realize.

❧

One of my favorite events on my calendar each year is the Global Leadership Summit, hosted by Bill Hybels and the Willow Creek Association. I love thinkers and thinking,

I crave the presence of thought leaders, and I am something of a conference junkie; so I sign up each year to go to this two-day conference. Of course the conference is for leaders and about leaders, and it's this great blend of the corporate and nonprofit world, public and private, Christian and secular, great and small. But the thing that always surprises me is how much of their masterful leadership content applies to parenting.

I don't know why this surprises me, since we parents are among the great leaders of the world, with the deepest influence to shape and alter lives on a grand scale. I guess I forget the parallels. Leadership just doesn't feel like the same game in the daily grind of stained library books and cereal bowls.

Which means that when Bishop T. D. Jakes sat down for his interview with Bill Hybels, I was not expecting this tremendous gem of wisdom for running a household: "I am never going to finish all the things I need to do. Something will go undone every day. If I do great in the workplace, I miss a dad moment. If I am great with the kids, I miss a husband moment. If I focus on my wife, I miss a work opportunity. I'll always miss something because there aren't enough hours in a day to get everything done. But the art of managing many things is to never drop the same thing two days in a row."[1]

Well.

Isn't that exactly true of all of us? At the end of every day, somebody somewhere in my circle of influence is going to go to bed disappointed. I could wrestle with this and beat myself up and lose sleep over lost time and opportunities, *or* I could take inventory of what I missed, realize that's how things go, and simply put them at the top of the list for tomorrow.

I will never be all that my children need, and I will disappoint them (and myself) with my mistakes. So while I'm spinning all the plates, confidence in parenting is not about *not dropping*. Drops happen. I need to aim only to never drop the same thing twice in a row. (Insert audible exhalation.) I feel like this is something I can do.

I have a friend whose daughter will never, ever let her forget that she had to call my friend's cell phone and ask her to please come *back* to Walmart and get her. Of course my friend was horrified to realize she'd left one of her children behind. But I think she should be congratulated for ensuring that she never left this young girl there again. And actually, she left behind none of her other kids, either. See there? A victory.

We all have twenty-four hours in a day. It's always been true of every single person, from the great leaders to the great squanderers. Many people have learned how to fit more into their day and ultimately their lives, but it's not because they had more time; it's because of how they focused their energy. You'll never be able to give all the priorities of your life equal time; it just doesn't work that way. But that cannot be an excuse for not regularly examining where you *do* invest your time and whether you're saving your best energy for the people and priorities that matter most to you. Perhaps too many of your resources are going in the wrong direction.

That's how we end up dropping the same plates again and again. If too much of your energy belongs to your work, then it may be time to evaluate and redistribute some of your energy.

∽

One evening recently, things had gone especially well with our night routine. Homework was finished early. We had hot dogs on the grill for dinner, and we made s'mores over the fire pit for dessert. There was conversation and authenticity in heaps. And everybody went to bed without ten thousand reasons to get back up. Because I'm prone to honesty with social media, and because I would likely write something quippy online to tell about my best-laid evening plans gone awry, I decided to do myself the equal favor and write that it had gone well. I wrote on Facebook: "What a perfect evening. I feel like a good mom tonight."

But my goodness, the responses made me so sad. A few dozen women commented with an overwhelming consensus: "I don't even know what that feels like." "I've never felt that way." "Must be nice."

Let's take a look at this for a minute. First of all, why are we so hard on ourselves and each other? I wasn't saying I had done everything perfectly, that we had scored an irrefutable touchdown in parenting and that now I shall post advice lists on Pinterest on how to plan your family times to be like mine. It's just that things came together, because sometimes they do. My personal gifts lean toward encouragement and affirmation, so when things go well—in my own life included—I am a big proponent of saying it out loud. I read these words from moms, and I thought, *Come on, girls. Surely you know what it's like to feel like a good mom now and then. Let's not be so hard on ourselves, so guilt-riddled that we've forgotten what a win looks like.*

On the other hand, if you're genuinely unhappy with how you're doing at this mom thing, if you really can't think of a time when you felt good at it, then change that. If you're feeling guilty in your parenting, ask yourself whether it's the real deal. Real guilt can be good and healthy when we look at it honestly. It can open the door to healing. Bring it out into the light and ask God to forgive you. By all means, ask your child to forgive you. After all, that's how they learn the cycle of vulnerability and forgiveness: by watching their parents.

But let's say you're parenting as well as you can, spinning the plates, trying not to drop them. How do you figure out what's really important when it comes to leading your children? How do you know where to put your focus on the parenting buffet? There is so much on the table: so many choices, so many categories, so much to teach and so little time.

I have to confess that sometimes my parenting is motivated by what I call the Daughter-in-Law Factor. I prioritize so I can minimize the inevitable apologies I'll owe to my future daughters-in-law. They'd like to marry men who pick up their socks, brush their teeth before bedtime, and know to look up from their devices when their wives talk to them. I find myself thinking, *I better cover that. His wife will want him to know that already,* even though my sons are nine and eleven. I don't want my future daughter-in-law to think, *Seriously? Did she teach him* nothing *in his first twenty-five years?* Never too soon to keep the end in mind, I contend. If this whole thing goes as fast as they say, then I'll hand him over to a wife before I know it. And I don't want to have to worry about his dirty dishes and clean underwear on his wedding day.

Along the way, on that journey of widowed single parenting, my daily teachable moments depended on my own bandwidth, on what kind of things I could handle. Honestly, for a lot of years, requiring the boys to help around the house was too overwhelming. In addition to actually doing the task, this battle required me to (a) train them to do it at all and then (b) follow up with consequences when they didn't do it. So often, I felt I could either gather my energy to train them *or* follow through with consequences, but not both. Parenting is a marathon, not a sprint, and I read that the ancient Greeks were rewarded not just for finishing the race but for finishing with their flame still burning. Sometimes I really do think that it's the daily following up with constant consequences that might just put my little flame right out.

So I felt like I needed to choose. Did I want (a) kids who were respectful and kind leaders in our family and their community or (b) kids who were responsible for doing their chores? I chose (a). It's not a bad portrait to paint, but the picture felt incomplete—especially with the Daughter-in-Law

Factor. As a result of choosing my battles, I discovered that I have children who are kind and respectful, who are great leaders in our family and in their community, and who don't do jack around the house.

But then, just as our house was about to collapse under the weight of undone chores, along came the new dad. Marrying a single mom is a different ball game, and Peter and I were twenty-four hours into our honeymoon when we realized we had never been alone for this many consecutive hours. We basked in seven days of uninterrupted conversation, knowing that our solitude would crash like cymbals the moment we got off the plane and stepped into our new life as parents together. Our honeymoon became something of a summit of like minds. We talked a lot about who we would become, what we wanted to define us as a couple and a family, and what values we wanted to implement upon our return. For the first time in a long time, I was not alone. A husband on my team fortified my authority and doubled my capacity as a parent. Suddenly, there was a new regime around here.

Peter's last name is Heyer (like "Higher"), and together we established a new routine for the boys: Heyer Expectations. (See what we did there?) They wake up each morning, check the refrigerator for their list of things to do, and cannot turn on any technology until those things are finished. In exchange for five days of Heyer Expectations, they turn in their lists on Saturday for $5.00 each. It's a good gig for all of us. The boys are learning how to manage some cash, and

I can sleep easier at night knowing that my daughters-in-law will have husbands who know how to empty the dishwasher. You're welcome, little ladies who are possibly barely able to comb your own hair at this point. I'm doing my part, keeping the end in sight.

We're all going to drop things. But the best thing about legacies is that they can be changed in an instant. I have a picture in my kitchen that says, "At any given point, you have the power to say, 'This is not how this story is going to end.'" Life doesn't give you a do-over, but you can claim a makeover. Pick something to do differently.

Claim it. Choose this day to be a confident mom.

## Stepping Forward

There are real things to feel guilty about, so there's no sense in wasting energy on the pretend ones. Choose today to be real with your kids, and choose to be fun. Bust out the cookies and milk, and have a picnic on the floor. After everybody puts their jammies on, pile them in the car for a late-night ice cream treat. Show them your silly side. Choose something simple and easy, and do it now. Do it today. I promise you: It will matter and the kids will remember. Restoration is a deep, wide pool of awesome.

CHAPTER 13

# Be Where You Are

*The Confident Girl Is Present and Engaged*

*Most humans are never fully present in the now, because unconsciously they believe that the next moment must be more important than this one. But then you miss your whole life, which is never not now.*

ECKHART TOLLE

**I WAS HOLDING** my friend's baby boy, a long-awaited newborn who was fifteen days old. He was wide-eyed, awake, and cuddly, and I was as smitten as I've always been with those perfect little newborn eyelashes and impossibly tiny fingernails. I swayed gently as we moms do, because putting a baby in our arms is like turning the crank on a windup toy. When Jack started to cry, I pulled out all my best newborn tricks, but then I remembered that sometimes the only thing a baby boy wants is his mama, not any fancy tricks from some lady who thinks she knows the drill. So I waved the white flag, and I handed that ten-pound sack of sugar back to his mommy. He quieted as soon as he heard the voice he had been listening to for nine months.

I watched their little reunion, and I remembered that sweetness with my own babies, when I was the only one they wanted and when we were each other's world. I remembered those earliest days when Robb and I were new parents, when we were staying up all night at the best slumber party ever, floating on the euphoric fact that together we had created a person.

And that's when I almost said, "Enjoy it. Enjoy every minute of this sacred season." Even now, recalling that sentiment makes me want to kick myself in the shins.

Thankfully, just before the words came spilling out of my mouth with the weight of a cliché that's a million years old, I remembered the truth: That season is sacred and fleeting, but it's not every-moment-enjoyable. That giddy stage I mentioned lasted roughly four nights, and then the sleepless hours caught up to us. We were unspeakably tired for a good many years.

As I listened to Jack's parents talk about how tired they were as they learned the likes and dislikes, needs and wants of this baby boy who is forever theirs, I stopped just short of saying those words I hate. The truth is, they will have some really great and unforgettable moments, but those moments might be scattered between some long stretches of really, really hard times.

As a mom, I know that sometimes a mother will be just so utterly exhausted that she can't see straight or think clearly. She'll have someone else's bodily fluids on her shirts for at least the next eight months. She's going to get peed on and pooped on. She'll add "go to the bathroom" to her list of things to do today, just so she can feel a measure of productivity. She'll cry a lot, and she won't know why. She will learn how tough she really is, how little sleep she really needs, and the subtle differences between her baby's hungry cry, his angry cry, and his scared cry. She will hear him learn his voice and her name. She will love him with a ferocity that could very well break her in half. She will wear her heart outside her body, from that day forward.

But it won't be easy or every-minute-wonderful. When my boys were toddlers, when I was Mom to two under three, when well-meaning grandmas would stop me in the grocery store and, calling out over the whining voices in my cart, remind me to "enjoy every moment" because I'll "miss it all someday," I remember thinking, *Will I miss this? Will I?*

I remember thinking, *I will miss the* next *stage. I will miss the preschool years, when they are potty-trained and a little independent, when we are having family movie night and game night and are reading books together and talking about what they are learning. I think I'll miss that.*

*I think I'll miss the elementary years, watching them run on the soccer field and be the blueberry in the school play. I think I'll miss the school projects (okay, maybe not the science fairs) and the family camping trips. I'll miss tucking them in and kissing them good night.*

*I think I'll miss the teenage years. I think I will miss their football games and halftime shows. I will miss their humor, when they will love to make me laugh against my best efforts* to keep a straight face. I think I will miss knowing and loving their friends, the bustle that comes with a houseful of teenagers hanging out after practice, eating everything in sight.

*But will I miss this? Will I?*

As I talked with my mom about all of this (as I so often do, since she knows this journey so well—she remembers its demands, and she doesn't make me feel ridiculous for feeling tired or spent), she said she would say the same thing differently. She doesn't miss the baby years, but she recalls them fondly. That's different. She looks at pictures of my brother and me, when we were so very little, and she remembers her babies. She even got teary saying so. Does she want to go back and do that again? No. Not at all. But her whole heart will always remember and hold dear those sweet little people who called her Mommy. There's a subtle difference there, and it's hidden in the sentiment every time someone tells new parents to enjoy it all.

That's refreshing. It's not about enjoying every minute; it's about enjoying the ones I can and making the most of the ones that are harder to embrace. (Like, oh, I don't know, the vomit in Tucker's bed this morning. Make the most of it, Tricia. Make the most of it.) I had been so incredulous when anyone told me I was going to miss this, while my children were hanging on my pant legs and demanding more, more, more. Maybe I will miss it someday, but for now, I'm just trying to survive.

But there is a closely related danger in the nature of survival: While I am waiting to "miss this," what if I really *miss this?*

What if I miss the little details that are my children, so small as they are today? What if I am so eager to move on and look back longingly that it all bypasses me in the moment? What if I miss the feel of their sweet little dimpled hands and their fingernails (which always need to be trimmed)? What if I don't look at them enough? What if I forget the feel of Tyler's hands in my hair, my curls gently tangled in his little fingers, as he falls asleep?

What if I forget the many faces of Tucker? He has a distinct expression when he is proud of himself, and when he is trying not to laugh, and when he knows he's funny. Three different smiles. What if I forget their subtle distinctions? What if I forget what it sounds like to hear them call my name, even if it feels incessant in the moment?

One year on my birthday, I gave myself the gift of sitting with them to watch *Sesame Street*, beginning to end. And to my surprise, I liked it. It was funny. But it was also darling, to sit in my chair with my little men. One on my lap, one at my side, all three of us wrapped up in Grover's silly antics. What if I don't do that enough, and when I'm finally ready to sit with them, they would rather run and play?

What if I forget how much Tyler loved his blanket? How he dove into it, in his crib, face first? What if I forget how they smell right after a bath (or even more endearing but challenging to love: right before the bath)?

What if I am so busy investing in other people that I forget to invest in them? What if all these calendar events called playdates are really just about me and the other moms, and

I'm just letting the boys tag along? What if I miss what they need from me today because I was too busy with the tasks of today? What if I let them slip through my fingers, when they were so briefly mine to hold? *What if I miss this?*

Okay, Tricia. Slow down. Yes, slow down with the questions and the what-ifs. But more importantly, just *slow down.* Slow down the schedule. Slow down the day. Let today be what it is instead of trying to fill it up, make it more, maximize. I have learned that discontentment sets in when I wish for *more.* More in my life, more in my day, more in this moment.

So that's the new plan. I am here. So are they. No regrets. I don't want to miss this. Because someday, I really, truly, actually might miss this. Be present where you are—in this moment, this day, this season, or this life stage. I think that's the secret to not longing for it later: Be fully present in it now.

I am so very thankful I caught myself just before I said those three words to that young couple in the trenches. Instead, I said, "I bet you're so tired, you guys. But I promise, you'll find your stride and you'll get some sleep again someday. It's okay if you don't love being awake in the middle of the night. That doesn't mean you don't love your baby; it just means you don't like being awake at ungodly hours." I rubbed my friend's tired shoulders, and I said, "Congratulations, weary mom. You are totally winning at this."

We are in a different life stage now, so different from the toddler-to-preschool years, and it's a season that's fulfilling and draining in different ways. I do feel as though I'm finding my stride, but sometimes, even in a season of intentional presence, I just have to get away and get lost. I just *have to*. It's part of being a good mom when I'm there—I just sometimes have to go away. (Because: boundaries.)

A few hours—or when you're fortunate, a couple of days—away from it all is exactly the Ctrl+Alt+Del to give a girl some perspective, a new approach, a new self-discovery, and a new plan. I went away for two days on a "digital cleanse." I escaped to the mountains and unplugged from everything.

Well, sort of. I unplugged from everything except this book I'm writing. And I didn't actually unplug my cell phone because nobody in our family can handle the inability to reach one another, and we can all chalk that up to PTSD. But I did stay off Facebook and my blog for forty-eight hours, and that, my friends, is not nothing.

I came back just before dinner on the second day, all refreshed and renewed and ready to be a hands-on mom again. I was going to take the boys out for dinner, hear about their days without me, tell them about mine, and as Tyler says, "just be joyful." But things didn't go quite that way.

I collected and doled out hugs and kisses. I counted freckles and measured how tall they'd grown because they always do when I'm not looking. And then I could immediately sense their awkward tension: They didn't want to hang out with me. They had stayed with my parents for a few days, and they really missed the baseballs and trampolines of our neighborhood.

They were trying to sort through that subtle message: *Mom, I love you, I'm glad you live here, and I'm so glad to see you. And you're not my entire life.*

*Touché, my boys. I love that you have lives and interests of your own, and I give myself two gold stars for fostering that right there. But the plan was dinner out. I'm still going out for dinner, by the way, with or without you.*

And so I doled out smooches and good-byes after about 0.2 seconds of touching home base. Cheers to well-adjusted children with great security in their environment and relationships, who understand that the anchor holds.

And one hour passed.

As I said, I still went out for dinner. But one hour later, they were ready to come back home before I had returned. All of a sudden, all of the slack in the heartstrings was too much for them. There was weeping and gnashing of teeth and feelings of *Mommy, get home now. And where were you and who said you could go anywhere and why weren't you home when we were ready for you?* There were tears and sadness and questions of priorities. We reviewed what I've been saying for years: "Guys, I'm here when you need me, and you do not always need me. We all had a plan, we knew the plan, and I always come back. See? Here I am."

There were exhalations of relief, and then: "Mommy, now that you're home, can we go back out to play?" Good grief. A girl could get whiplash with the back-and-forth of it all.

Therein lies the balance of parenting and independence: letting them run free within boundaries and curfews, and yet staying close enough to be there when they're ready to come home. It's the whole idea of roots and wings.

Oh, and by the way, while you're holding the string to their kite as they soar in the breeze, keep your heart solid and confident enough to balance the tension of learning whether your presence is necessary, whether it's preferred, or whether it's just best for you to take a step back. Parenting is not for the insecure or the faint of heart.

Before my children ran out to play yet again, there was a quivering chin and a gentle voice: "Mommy, I just don't want you to think that somebody else is more important to me than you are."

Sweet boy. It's not your job to make me feel important. I said, "Buddy, I don't feel that way. Listen to these words, okay? We make a great team. You can spend time doing other things with other people, and we will still be a great team. Our family is tight and important to each other, and we can love other people, too. We love other people differently than we love each other, and that's absolutely okay. Sometimes I spend time doing other things with other people, whether I'm writing or working or having dinner with a grown-up. You might feel sometimes like I love someone else more than you guys, but I want you to know this: I will love them differently than I love you, and we will still make a great team."

"Mom, you've said that like nineteen times now. Can I just go play?"

(Does it ever happen to you that you're so busy imparting wisdom, you don't realize their eyes have glazed over?)

Just like that, the breeze picked up, the kite of independence pulled, and I loosened the string once again.

Later on, when I look back on this life stage, or when I look at someone else in the throes of it, I know that I know that I know I'll be tempted to say it, to tell them all to enjoy every single minute. But confidence isn't dependent on enjoying every minute; confidence lives in the space of letting the moment breathe, letting it be what it is, even if you don't love the sleepy stickiness of it. So I hope I'll filter my words and instead I'll say what I really mean: "Be where you are, dear one. You're winning at this."

## Stepping Forward

What is the "now" season of your parenting? Decide to lean into it with purpose. Sure, our children love playing on technology—but they've heard about Monopoly and chess and even rummy, and that can be an evening of great fun too. Change it up by tossing a deck of cards into your purse and playing at the food court in the mall instead of at home. Go make some memories. Almost all of us have a silly or adventurous side, though we may have buried it under adult responsibilities. Pull it out on purpose, and do the unexpected. Even if you have to plan it and make it *look* unplanned.

In her book *The Happiness Project*, Gretchen Rubin offered these seven tips for being a more lighthearted parent:

1.  Laugh! At least once a day, make each child
    helpless with laughter.

2.  Sing in the morning. It's hard both to sing and
    to maintain a grouchy mood.

3.  Get enough sleep yourself.

4.  Most messages to kids are negative: "Stop," "Don't,"
    "No." Try to say Yes. "Yes, we'll go as soon as you've
    finished eating."

5.  Say No only when it really matters. Wear a bright red
    shirt with bright orange shorts? Sure. Put water in the
    toy tea set? Okay.

6.  Repetition works . . . with kids, so use the school
    mantras: "Sit square in your chair" and "You get what
    you get, and you don't get upset."

7.  Remember: The age of Cheerios and the Tooth Fairy is
    fleeting. The days are long, but the years are short.[1]

If you're past the trenches of parenting babies and toddlers,
do you ever need a "baby fix"? Call up a young mom and
give her a break. Offer to care for her little guys for a while,
or schedule a turn in your church's nursery. (A few rounds
of spit-up and messy diapers might just help you put it all
back in perspective!)

Make your technology work for you. Use your phone to
document this season, and then take it to the next step:
Get prints made. (There are apps that offer free prints—you

pay only for shipping, and the memories come right to your door.) Plenty of pictures can jog your memory in a few years when this day, this season, might otherwise fade into black and white.

# CHAPTER 14

# Wait for the Timer to Beep

## *The Confident Girl Doesn't Overreact*

*Mom, if I go down, I'd like for you to take out your phone, and set a timer for five minutes. You have to promise me you won't step onto the football field until those five minutes are up.*

MY SON TUCK, AGE ELEVEN

**MY SON TUCKER WAS** born with a love for football coursing through his veins. Any sport with a ball comes unbelievably naturally to him, but his heart beats for football. I signed him up for flag football as soon as he was old enough, and I embraced the role of football mom with everything in me. I even have a blinged-out T-shirt with a sparkly football on it and glittery letters that say, "He got it from his mom." Which is laughably untrue, and I wear it purely for irony.

I delayed the transition from flag football into tackle for as long as possible, protecting his body and his brain with the illusion of my control, until even his flag coaches were telling me it was time. He has the elements of the game. This boy *needs* to *tackle.* I waited until we had Peter firmly in position as new dad, in-home coach, and Master of Identifying Appropriate Leagues and Stocking Equipment, and I finally gave the green light. I think it sounded something like "Yes, let's do this. It's time. I think. Wait. No, let's do this. Sign him up before I change my mind."

We were shopping for his equipment, which is no small situation and no small price tag, and I needed to take a knee for the sticker shock of it all. Peter was talking with the sales guy about items that included words like *air bladder* and *girdle* and *cup,* and I was thankful to not be the one navigating those conversations. In the next aisle with my son, I said, "Tuck, could you help me with something?"

I put my arm around him; he put his arm around me. "Sure, Mom."

"Would you please coach me on *what on earth* I am to do when you fall down hurt on the field?"

He turned to face me. I had opened a window for a conversation he very obviously wanted to have.

"Yes. Here's what you should do. If I go down, I'd like for you to take out your phone, and set a timer for five minutes. You have to promise me you won't step onto the field until those five minutes are up. If five minutes goes by and nobody has helped me yet, then quietly let my coach know."

"*Five minutes?*"

"Five minutes."

"That's a long time, buddy."

"I know, Mom. But you have to let me handle this."

Which is pretty much everything there is to say in eleven words.

And then he said, "If it's emergent" (he actually used the word *emergent*, which admittedly made me a little weak in the knees because I have a thing for vocabulary words), "then I'll pound on my chest twice and give you the peace sign. Then you'll know I need you."

Right. I'll watch for that subtle mom cue. Because if he's actually seriously injured and actually needs his mom, then I'm sure that three-step signal will actually come right to his mind. I'm absolutely confident it will go down this way.

"But Mom, seriously. Just wait for the timer to beep."

His logic kind of blew me away. *Basically, Mom, let's agree you won't charge the field until the timer beeps, and then you still won't. Deal?* And I know all too well that if I charge the field before the allotted time and against the plan he has instituted, he'll have no problem lecturing me, "Mom. We talked about this."

At the first practice we met his new coach, who shook Tucker's hand and said, "So, you've played flag football for a few years? Well done, kid. Welcome to the team. Now let's have some real fun." I watched his team come over to fist-bump and chest-plow their new teammate. I watched my son take the field and fade into their solidarity. I watched him join the brotherhood.

I stood by the sidelines and watched him run drills, careful not to embarrass him with my very presence. But I kept my sunglasses on to hide the sudden tears. I just felt thankful.

Thankful that he could walk, since just one year before he had undergone a total reconstructive surgery after a terrible fall from a swing set when he crushed the arch of his foot. If we lived in another part of the world, my son wouldn't have been able to walk again after such a debilitating accident. Sometimes I have to stop, take a moment, and thank the Lord for medicine and doctors and the luxury of solutions.

I felt thankful to stand on the sidelines next to Peter, the brave man who claims my sons as his own, who has confidently walked us into this subculture of helmets and jerseys. I felt thankful that I was not alone. And I felt thankful to watch my son living the dream he'd had from the moment he held a ball in his chubby little toddler hands.

The truth is, being a football mom has become one of my favorite gigs. I'm all about the muddy car, empty refrigerator, full Saturdays, and tired lungs. I have learned to smell the fear and feel the pride. I wash the uniform and stock the Gatorade. I drive to practices and clean the wounds. Some people have to wait their entire lives to meet their favorite player. I'm raising mine.

As I thought later about that conversation with Tucker in the sports equipment aisle, I realize how much wisdom he had handed to me: the art of the delayed response. I read somewhere that former US president Harry Truman had a personal policy: Any letters written in anger had to sit on his desk for twenty-four hours before he put them in the mail. If at the end of that cooldown period he still felt the same strong sentiments, he sent the letter. But very often, his temper cooled, and he chose to respond differently. By the end of his life, it is said that Truman's unmailed letters filled a large desk drawer. I like to imagine the immeasurable relationships, conversations, and dignity spared by that desk drawer of delayed responses. Choosing to delay the response is still, in fact, a decision.

Tuck had this advice he intended me to follow all mapped out for me quite completely, and the steps for his action plan were actually transferrable for almost any maybe-crisis, the kind that is possible but may never happen. He had put together a pretty foolproof plan for the confident girl to not overreact, and his plan applies across the board to every crisis I can imagine. Even if I can't quite hold out for the entire five minutes.

## Stepping Forward

Create your plan.

1.  Identify what could go wrong or what is scaring you. It could be anything across a broad spectrum: a child getting injured or sick, your husband getting fired, your family dissected by conflict, a car accident, something as small as an argument with someone or as large as a natural disaster. I won't go on because I'm pretty sure you don't need me to.

2.  Choose calm. Decide in advance that you will keep yourself in hand and you will not allow panic to overtake you. Yes. You *can* make such decisions

in advance. It's actually one of the best ways you can prepare.

3.  Decide on a plan for how you will patiently choose not to overreact. It may be a timer on your phone or a date on the calendar, depending on the type of crisis. Know that your patience is not a lack of response but rather a decision to be still.

4.  When that determined time has passed and it's now time to react, decide to let your next step be small and subtle, asking someone nearby for help.

5.  When it's time to be bold, then by all means be bold. Sometimes a situation calls for a quick response, a confident voice, difficult words, and a firm decision. When that need arises, be the woman who can handle it. That is confidence in its finest hour.

# CHAPTER 15

# The Underbelly of Confidence

### The Confident Girl Chooses Vulnerability

*I spent a lot of years trying to outrun or outsmart vulnerability by making things certain and definite, black and white, good and bad. My inability to lean into the discomfort of vulnerability limited the fullness of those important experiences that are wrought with uncertainty: Love, belonging, trust, joy, and creativity to name a few.*

BRENÉ BROWN

**SO HERE'S THE TRUTH, THOUGH.** There is one downside to being a confident woman. When you're confident in who you are and what you bring to the world, sometimes the people around you may feel like you don't need them. When independence comes easily, or even if it eventually comes at all, then the people who want you to depend on them can feel displaced. And it's not a good feeling for anybody involved. A confident girl needs her people, and sometimes she needs to rely on their strength.

A couple of weeks before our wedding, Peter and I were in

a funk. Nothing that puts a wedding at risk, but just a little bit off. Now, first of all, let's just acknowledge that it's easy to feel off center in the final days before a wedding. I contend that being engaged is *the worst*. It puts you in a constant state of transition, and transition is the most painful place to be. I'd rather be on one side of the fence or the other. Straddling it makes me irritable and uncomfortable. We were in that weird in-between place where we were no longer dating but not yet married. We were ready to floor it right into the next life stage, but we were stuck in neutral. Our gears were grinding.

I think one of the best things we have going for us is that we each have a finger on the pulse of our emotional intimacy, and we both prefer studying the situation head-on instead of with a cowardly sideways glance, hoping it goes away on its own. If something is even slightly off, we practically race against each other to be the first to identify it. We have a strict policy against any invisible animals in our relationship: If there's an elephant in the room or a monkey on my back or his, then we're going to name that sucker and escort it right out the front door. I knew there was a problem, and I leaned hard into finding out what it was.

It took a little time, because as intentional as we are, the person who is upset spends a fair amount of time trying to pretend there's nothing wrong. Peter didn't want there to be anything wrong, and it bothered him that I knew he was bluffing. I get that entirely. Sometimes it's annoying when there's nowhere to hide. I sat him down and invited him to just tell me. "Babe, what is going on?"

And out came this little and beautiful packaged gift of vulnerability. He said, "I feel like you don't need me."

"Oh, of course I do," I said. I linked my arm through his, tickled his arm with my fingernails, flirting with him and leaning hard on my cute to win his mood. But there comes a moment in every relationship—and in the hardest conversations—where cute doesn't work. It's maddening when you realize that trump card holds no value. Still, a girl can try. "I need lots of things about you, babe."

He wasn't buying it. "No, Trish. You actually don't."

I looked at him, this man who had become my anchor. He was the start to my morning and the end of my day. He had become the parentheses around my scattered thoughts. He is one who asks the best questions, who chases after my heart so incessantly. The one who makes my coffee exactly the way I love it, who reads books with me, who holds my hand and makes sure I walk on the inside of the sidewalk, who shares the ice cream spoon and the phone charger in the car. (These are not small things.) He knows my story and my secrets, and he was quickly becoming the best part about me. I looked at his silver hairline, his strong jawline, and I wondered how in the world I had let him feel like I didn't need him.

But then, on the one hand, he had a point. I didn't *need* him. He had come into my life on the very last leg of a journey I had nearly given up. I had just come out of a terribly dark valley that had been several years deep. See, when Robb died, I became exceedingly needy. I needed a lot of people in a lot of ways. I needed my parents to hold my seams together. I needed my sister-friends to keep me from drowning. I needed every meal that my community magically provided in the cooler we left on the front porch. I needed hours of silence every day. I needed to sleep for two-thirds of every twenty-four hours. I needed to borrow other people's faith and courage and confidence because mine had all been stripped away. But slowly, in the deep end of my life, I began to learn how to float on my own, even if I was too tired to swim. Each day, I got a little bit stronger, a little bit braver, a little bit more of a brand-new version of myself. I began to not need so much. And if I'm honest, as I reflect on my self-preservation, as I began to understand life on my own, I think part of me resolved to just *not need* anymore. I decided I would establish a new life with my own work, my own money, my own fortitude. Something in me needed to not need.

I looked at Peter's honest vulnerability, and I held it with both hands. I loved him even more than I had just moments before. But I didn't necessarily want to trade in my independence card for a marriage license. I wanted Peter to see my hard-earned independence—this not-neediness—as a wonderfully attractive thing about me.

I said, "But isn't it freeing to marry a girl who doesn't *need* you? Sure, I don't *need* to do life with you, but I just *want* to. How wonderful to just be wanted. Isn't it? Wonderful?"

I thought I had offered him a perfect solution, a perfect freedom. He didn't have to fix anything or provide anything or be anything but himself. I wanted him to just be. With me. Just be with me.

I nudged his elbow, my voice softer this time. "Please say it's wonderful, Pete."

But he said, "All I can tell you is that a man needs to be needed. And you don't need me."

Part of me wanted to turn on the waterworks, the damsel-in-distress routine, and let him be the hero. But I knew in the most honest part of me that such antics would only patronize both of us. I would violate all of my personal policies about being smart and confident, about not making myself smaller so I could make someone else feel bigger. He was right. I didn't need him, not in the ways he wanted to be needed. I had to let that truth lie there, even if it would have been momentarily easier and perhaps more attractive to be a wispy waif who would float away on the breeze were it not for a knight to hold on to her. It seemed easier to pretend I'm someone I'm not, but that would do no favors for the marriage we were days from entering. We both had to know what we were getting into with our eyes wide open. Anything else was a lie to each other and to ourselves.

Sometimes you just have to let people feel how they feel, and sometimes you have to acknowledge truth and then move on because things need doing, like laundry and baths and bedtimes and dishes. So I took his truth, and I simply received it for what it was: an honest gift that was hard to hold.

That night, before the boys' bedtime, we read that day's

passage in a daily app on my iPad: *Jesus Calling for Kids*. I want to tell you it happens every night, but I'd say we're on a two-out-of-seven-nights weekly average. But I have to say, Sarah Young has a direct hotline to the voice of Jesus, I'm pretty sure. Her writing is anointed and sacred, and the Word of God is alive in her words. Anytime we commit to reading this together, Jesus meets us there. And I was not prepared in any way for the tidal wave that would hit our family that night.

We sat on the couch in my family room, Peter and me beside each other with the boys sprawled across the coffee table and ottoman. I reminded myself that God doesn't mind bad posture and sloppy living rooms, and we passed the iPad to Tucker, our first reader of the night. (I read somewhere that you should read important messages and letters twice aloud: the first time for your head, the second for your heart.) Tuck read to us:

> *For as the heavens are higher than the earth, so are My ways higher than your ways, and My thoughts than your thoughts.* —Isaiah 55:9 (NKJV)
>
> I gave you an amazing mind. With it you can think great thoughts and dream great dreams. But My Mind is infinitely bigger and more amazing. My thoughts contain all of creation and the universe, all of the past, present, and future. And because I understand all things and all times, My thoughts and My ways are different from yours.

Life can be like a box of puzzle pieces—with the box top missing. When you look around at your life, all you can see are the pieces. But I see the final picture. I know how all the pieces fit together. I know how to join together all the jagged pieces of hurts and disappointments, plus the smooth pieces of victories and joys.

Trust My timing and My ways. Trust Me to fit all your pieces together into a wonderful life. And trust Me—at the end of your life—to lead you home to heaven.[1]

He passed the iPad to Tyler, and as the second reading soaked into my heart, I felt tears fill my eyes. Peter and I were holding hands, sending little squeezes in the back-and-forth way we do that says, *This is big right now. What we're seeing and hearing, this is big. We have to talk about this.*

Tyler finished reading, and I said, "Oh my goodness, you guys. This is so perfect tonight. Here we are, just a few days before I marry Peter, just before we are a family of four, and I can see so clearly right now that God has had his hand on us all along. I think back to those nights after your dad died, when I was so very sad. More sad than I can ever even explain to you. And I would put you to bed, my little tiny boys, and once you were asleep, I would lie in my bed and ask God where he was. I would ask him what he was letting happen to us, what he had in mind for my little children, and why he thought this was a good idea. And now I see—tonight, as we read this together, now that we are healed and becoming whole—I can see now that he was with us all along."

I thought my moment of revelation would be such a gift to them. I thought they would also see what I could see on the heels of our long journey. I thought it would be a comforting, teachable moment. But instead my son started to cry. He cried the sobs of a growing boy who hasn't yet given himself over to becoming a young man. Peter was sitting closest to him, and he put his arm around my sobbing son. As we waited and listened to learn what was going on in his mind, I realized how very polarized these two topics are: the morning Robb died, coupled with the healing gift of Peter in our lives. It was too much, too hot to hold.

With Peter safely between us, my son unraveled the knots of his thoughts. We talked about the morning when his "first dad" died. My son said that morning was like a movie in his mind, except there was no sound. He remembered when I carried him out to my friend's car in the driveway, how he didn't have time to put on his shoes, how he had to squeeze into the little toddler car seat in her backseat because that's all the room there was. He remembered a policeman waving to him as we carried him out to the car. He remembered the lights of all the police cars, ambulances, and fire trucks. He recalled vivid images, but none of the conversations of that frightening morning. He couldn't understand why I had arranged for him to leave, he didn't think anyone had tried to help him understand, and he felt I hadn't answered his questions.

The thing about childhood trauma is that the loss grows and changes with the child's own cognitive ability. As my children learn more about life, they understand more about loss. I realized we were at a new crossroads, and it was time for a new conversation.

I said, "Sweetheart, ever since the day your dad died, I have told you everything I could tell you. But you were only five years old, so there was only so much you could understand. But I promise you, from that day forward, I have answered every question you've asked me, always with information you could handle for how old you were. As you have grown, I could tell you more, and as you continue to grow, I'll keep telling you more. What would you like to know?"

He took a deep breath. "Mom, tell me what it was like. For you."

And so I told him. I took a deep breath too, and I told him what that morning was like before the sun came up, just two days before Christmas. I told him how his dad called me for help, how I came running as fast as I could, and how I called 911, begging for help. I told him what his dad looked like, the color of his face as he died, different from any shade in the Crayola box. I told him what that last breath sounded like, as if someone had sat down on his chest and pushed the last gust of air out of him. I told him how my stomach still drops exactly the same way it did when I let myself recall the moment when I realized this was it, the end: the last moment I would see his dad alive. I told him how it had seemed like winter for so many months, even when the sun was shining. And I told him how I had felt like I was drowning in sadness but had worked really hard to keep doing the next thing because I had two children who deserved everything I could give them. And I told him how sometimes I woke up in the night to find three-year-old Tyler's soft baby blanket spread over me. It was his greatest comfort, and he couldn't sleep without it; it was a precious offering he gave to me while I was sleeping. I told him how people came to help us, bringing us food and cleaning the house and keeping groceries in the cupboards and joy in our home, and I told him how the three of us—my boys and me—became an incredible team. I told him that I had learned how strong we are, that we can do hard things.

The irony was not lost on me, the fact that Tuck could only now talk about these things with Peter here to comfort him and to sit in between us, to be the buffer between his broken heart and his mom's tears, to take care of his heart and hold him together. My son could finally ask the hard questions he needed to voice, now that there was someone, a man stronger than we were, between us. The words could hit Peter before they hit me, and my sadness could fall on Peter before it fell on Tucker. There are things a growing young man needs his dad to do, ways he needs to protect his own mom. Peter was becoming my son's new dad, right before my eyes.

We were learning—all of us together—about the heart's endless capacity to love. We were learning that people are not replaceable but that the absence of one can lead to the gift of another. We were learning that it's possible to feel sad and happy at the same time, that joy and sorrow are sisters who travel together in the same moments. It's all so complicated, even for an adult. We stepped into the conversations, and I remembered again that my children are some of the bravest individuals I know.

My son listened to me, word for word. We matched each other, courage for courage. My fiancé sat between us, listening to us. Peter held each of our hands, holding us together. I knew implicitly that this was one of those moments written in bold letters, a moment that matters, a moment that defines.

And then Tucker said, "Okay. Thanks for telling me, Mom. Can we be done now?"

I have learned the key to all these hard, vulnerable, transparent, remembering conversations: I let my children decide when to start and when to finish. Tuck asked his questions, got his answers, felt heard, and then was finished. It isn't always a smooth decrescendo; sometimes it's just the end.

We prayed together once more before he left his place on the couch. He said, "And God, thank you for this smart, strong, independent woman. Thank you that she's my mom. Amen."

And I silently realized, *Oh dear God, he gets it.*

There's a risk in letting your kids see too much, in letting them peek behind the curtain of vulnerable parenting.

There's a risk in letting them see the weak points. But sometimes that's what a confident woman must do: She must be vulnerable. I had let my son see the soft side of my strength, the jagged truth of how my heart had broken. And instead of seeing weakness, he found the words *smart, strong,* and *independent*. If he can see this in his own mom, then he's well on his way to looking for these qualities in his own wife someday, the woman who will be the mom to his children. And so I echoed my son: "Amen, Lord. Amen."

I watched him walk up the stairs to bed, so keenly aware that he didn't need any bedtime help from me anymore. He didn't need help with his jammies, with brushing his teeth, with filling his water bottle, or even with a bedtime story. He was growing up and away from me. It didn't make me sad; I simply felt aware. Sharply, keenly aware of this profound moment. He walked up the stairs, and the day was done.

Here's what I know about myself. I can do hard things, because sometimes you don't know how strong you are until you have no choice. I had spent a good many years having no choice. In the face of the hard thing, I will keep my game face and *get it done*. I've learned this so implicitly that I even have a mantra I whisper in moments of grace under fire: "You can absolutely cry about this later. But right now, Trish, I need you to stay in the game." And then I can promise you this: Shortly after the crisis, when the boys are asleep or away, when the room is quiet and nobody needs me to be strong, when I have a couple inches of margin to lay down my shield? Well, my friends, *that* is when I'll fall to pieces. The anxiety will rise in waves, and I'll get swept away on the current of a panic attack.

In all our months together, Peter had not yet seen this kind of unleashed anxiety. He had seen glimpses of anxiety, even some of the tremors that come with my remembering. But he had not yet experienced the catatonic state I slip into, the seizure-like tremors and the inability to respond. I hadn't let that happen in front of him. Not yet. But just like children get to decide when the hard conversations happen, PTSD gets to decide when panic hits and just how hard. The floodgates opened, the adrenaline flooded my system, and I knew what I know: I could only hold on and wait for it to run its course. I've ridden this storm so many times since the morning Robb died. This time, I held on to Peter.

My hands shook, and I clenched my fists. My body seized into rhythmic tremors. Peter sat with me, holding me, rocking me. I couldn't talk, but I could listen. He talked to me as I writhed uncontrollably.

He said, "You did a great job, honey. You are brave and strong, and I'm so proud of you. You answered some hard questions, and you had to go to dark places. You did a great job, babe. You're okay. Tuck is safe, and so are you. I'm right here."

In a panic attack, I curl into a tight ball. My hands ball into tight fists, and I hold them by my chin while my body shakes in a fetal position. Peter lay down to face me, wrapping his arms around my body. He let my panic rage against his calm. He stayed so still and steady, talking to me, breathing with me, letting me feel his arms around me.

And then he did something completely revolutionary in the face of my raging panic. As we lay face to face with his arms around me, my balled fists were next to his chin. Without a word, he gently worked his chin into my clenched fist until he found the palm of my hand, and he gently unfurled my fist with his bearded chin. He straightened my fingers and opened my palm, all without using his hands. With my palm open, he stroked his chin from my palm to my fingertips, back and forth, back and forth, back and forth. I can't explain the science of sensory therapy, but something about his prickly chin against my skin pushed a reset button in my mind. The rhythms of his movement and the texture of his beard quieted me and gave my mind something to think about, an anchor to hold on to. My body began to relax, my breathing began to slow, and I began to calm. Without using his hands or even his voice, he soothed me.

He helped me to my bedroom, and he stayed with me until I was nearly asleep that night. He tucked my covers up to my chin, and he kissed my forehead.

And then he said to me, so gently, "Hey, honey? I think you need me."

"I do, Peter. In more ways than you'll ever know."

And then, as he closed my bedroom door, I heard him whisper so simply, "Thanks, God."

# Stepping Forward

A confident girl needs her people. Think of the people in your life whom you need the most. Send them a text, a Facebook message, or—my favorite—a handwritten note. Make sure they know how you need them, count on them, and live your best life because they're in this with you.

If you fear that you don't have people, set out to find them. The most surefire way is to be the person whom others need, whom they can rely upon to care, to love, to feel what they're feeling, and to simply be there. Watch for small ways to strengthen friendships, one thread at a time, until a strong and unbreakable cord is formed. It takes time—and it's worth your investment.

CHAPTER 16

# Put Fear in the Backseat

*The Confident Girl Refuses Fear*

*The one thing necessary is courage, for strength without self-confidence
is useless.*

GIACOMO CASANOVA

**SOMETIMES,** on the best days, happiness feels too good to be
true. Sometimes I feel like I'm living between the parentheses
of a sentence I can't see, and I can easily convince myself that
surely some darkness is hiding around the corner of whatever
joy I'm experiencing right now. This is the story of my life
sometimes, the terrible and forever twin residents of joy and
fear. These two emotions seem to counteract and activate
one another. Whenever things are going well, I inevitably
fear that something must be about to go wrong. Does this
ever happen to you?

I'm a hearty, note-taking student of Brené Brown, as you
may have noticed by the sheer number of times I have quoted
her. I like to think of myself as one of her graduate students,

auditing all her courses long distance. (And of course, we're on a first-name basis in my healthy imagination.) Brené says that joy is probably the most difficult emotion to feel, that when we lose the ability or the willingness to be vulnerable, joy becomes something we approach with deep foreboding.

Foreboding: The feeling that something bad will happen.[1]

Joy: A feeling of great happiness.[2]

Yes. I am the very picture of this.

Brené says,

> Joy can feel like a setup. . . . We're always waiting for the other shoe to drop. We're trying to beat vulnerability to the punch. We don't want to be blindsided by hurt. We don't want to be caught off-guard, so we literally practice being devastated. . . . We've learned that giving in to joy is, at best, setting ourselves up for disappointment and, at worst, inviting disaster.[3]

Her words resonate deeply with the widowed part of me. (I say "part of me" because I resist being solely defined as a widow. The word carries too much shrouding and darkness. But the word is part of who I am, an important chapter of my story, and a scar that will always be tender even if it's no longer a bleeding wound.) I know firsthand how it is to be blindsided not only by the pain of losing my husband but also by the shock of instant solo parenting of my two small boys with life rushing past every day. How could my heart stand the thought of trying to live through the reality of a true nightmare, now that I've experienced one?

As I was writing this paragraph, Peter called to tell me the results of his physical. He said, "Honey, buckle up, because you may get more than you bargained for. The doctor said I am completely healthy, and I'll probably live into my nineties." I literally gasped on the phone. This excellent bill of health prompted a sure response from me: a quick intake of air and then the demanding whisper, "Shhh. Please don't say that."

And then tears. The act of telling me he is healthy only made me sure he won't be for long. And so I practiced my own devastation. I hate living in this vice. There is a dark and fearful part of me that believes God takes away the things I love. *I cannot fall in love with him*, I used to think. *God will take him away*. It isn't true, of course. And yet it kind of was, once.

I want to just run and jump into this next season of my life with the same gusto as when I used to run and jump into a playland ball pit as a little girl. I was sure the balls would catch me in a soft balloon landing, so I'd run and close my eyes and leap, delighting in the big splashy rainbow that swallowed me whole. I want that abandoned leaping again.

Brené says there is one cure: gratitude.

She says that none of us is immune to that uncomfortable quake of vulnerability that accompanies joyful moments. But the most experienced among us have learned to use that shudder of vulnerability as an invitation to acknowledge how truly grateful we are for the person, the beauty, the connection, or simply the moment before us. You can't keep bad things from happening. You can only be thankful that it's not right now. And then, says Brené, when the bad things happen, you've strengthened your own fortitude to handle it.

So let me get this straight: Practicing my own devastation doesn't actually prepare me for it. Instead, joy and gratitude strengthen my own resilience. I have to say, it's hard to believe. I don't know how all of this can work for me and not against me.

With phone still in hand, I sat up tall, determined to get a handle on this. I took a deep breath that felt like determination with ragged edges. I looked up as Peter walked into the restaurant and over to the table where I was writing that day, some place with free wi-fi and endless refills for my Diet Coke. He had left the doctor's office and driven across town to the tears he'd heard dripping on the phone. He sat down, and he was so tender with me, which nearly broke me in a different way.

"Honey, what's happening? What are you feeling?" he asked.

Tearfully, I said, "I'm feeling . . . thankful."

It's a choice, and it's a hard one. But it's one I get the opportunity to make often, because fear—the other choice—is never very far away. The truth is that a confident woman must choose to refuse to give fear a voice. It doesn't mean that you don't feel fear, but it means that you're choosing not to listen to it or be paralyzed in its control. Fear is present, but it doesn't rule your decisions and actions.

⁂

Even if you're not consumed with possible loss, you might be—brace yourself—an *artist*. If you're an artist, you must become especially comfortable with the presence of fear; it's part of the process. Choosing to live creatively brings along an invitation to nearly constant fear. They live together. As a writer, my creative mind is constantly at work against me: What if I say something people don't agree with? What if I don't get it right? What if I *do* get it right? What if they totally love it, and then I have to somehow maintain that standard of writing things that people love and agree with? In Elizabeth Gilbert's book *Big Magic*, she paints this gloriously true and accurate word picture of the act of living with fear. Essentially, she says that fear and creativity are conjoined twins and that fear is kind of like a family member that just needs to be included. So on the road trip of life, you have to set ground rules for the passengers. Here's what she says to fear:

> You're allowed to have a seat, and you're allowed to
> have a voice, but you are not allowed to have a vote.
> You're not allowed to touch the road maps; you're
> not allowed to suggest detours; you're not allowed to
> fiddle with the temperature. Dude, you're not even
> allowed to touch the *radio*. But above all else, . . . you
> are absolutely forbidden to drive.[4]

I love how she says that! If you don't leave room for fear, then you'll only feel frustrated and scared when it shows up again. Instead, just expect it. Besides, fear can be good. It means you're doing something really, really brave.

In Matthew 25:14-30, Jesus told the parable of the three

servants. In this parable a master gives three of his servants some money, each according to his abilities. I especially love this story in relation to artists, since many translations tell us that the master gives them "talents." In their day, a talent was a unit used to weigh gold or silver, but it's wonderfully simple to think of the word in our terms, to measure skills and abilities. The master gives them each their talents, and then he leaves. When he comes back, he asks them to show what they did with what he gave them. The first two used their talents to gain more, but the third servant kept his talents hidden for fear of losing them altogether. We read that the master was so pleased with the first two guys, but he's bitterly disappointed in the third. In fact, the master takes the talents away from the third servant and gives them to the first two. Again, I'm reminded that this story is about money; still, it's easy to imagine that my skills and abilities could easily go to somebody else if I'm too fearful to use what I have. Jesus said, "Whoever can be trusted with very little can also be trusted with much."[5] He's given us a starting point, and he's waiting to see what we'll do with it. Faithfulness is multiplying what you've already been given, and this kind of multiplication takes courage.

Confidence and negativity are like oil and water. You can't be brave while you're telling yourself you can't do it, and you can't have courage when you're telling yourself all the things that can go wrong. If we draw back in fear, God does not delight in us. Now, don't freak out over this, because here's what that does not mean: *It doesn't mean that he doesn't love us.* He loves us always and forevermore, not in spite of who we are but because of whose we are, and that's never in question. But when we draw back in fear, he feels disappointed because he knows he had something incredible in mind and we are the ones who will miss out.

I kind of understand this from a parenting perspective. I love to plan fun things to do with my kids on our days together. I can pack a picnic that will give you butterflies of anticipation in your hungry stomach, and I can pack some serious adventures into a day. My children rarely draw back in fear, but sometimes they can throw things off with bad attitudes. More than once, I've found myself saying, "You guys, you're ruining this day. Don't you know I wanted to do something fun with you? I had great things in store, and now my crazy-awesome plans are delayed—or, God help us, *canceled*—because you're making things difficult." (It's not a good situation for anyone when my adventures are on hold. I get grumpy. Proverbial heads roll.)

I wonder how often God has thought of saying that to me: "Tricia, I have such great plans for you, and I'm so disappointed that you're kind of being a punk right now. You're letting fear win, and that disappoints me. I'm disappointed that you'll miss out on the adventure and the intimacy with me, but it's your choice. Go ahead and be afraid, but know that I wanted more for you."

Here's a very important truth about courage: It isn't always big. I have a magnet on my refrigerator with a quote from Mary Anne Radmacher that says, "Courage doesn't always roar. Sometimes courage is the quiet voice at the end of the day saying, 'I will try again tomorrow.'"[6] For most of my life, and especially during my years as a single mom, that was what the whole journey was about. Sometimes it has been about saying, "Well, that's not what I had in mind, but I'll try again tomorrow." I read somewhere that each day gives us two gifts: the ability to start fresh at the beginning of the day and the ability to put it all behind us when we go to bed. Sometimes courage simply says, *Yep. I'm here again. Trying again. In my small, brave way.*

The life God calls us to is not a safe life. We can ask Joseph, Moses, Abraham, Deborah, Esther, and Ruth. We can ask Mary, Lazarus, Peter, James, and John. We can ask modern-day martyrs who lost their lives in the wake of fierce persecution. The Old and New Testaments are filled with people whom God called to dangerous lives. I don't believe they were victorious over fear, but they must have overcome the voice of it. God wants greatness for us, and greatness is born of courage.

I am a collector of encouragements, most often in quotations, words, and verses. One of my favorite verses says that God has not given me a spirit of fear.[7] I love the absolute nature of it in the face of uncertainty. There aren't a lot of things in life that I can know for sure, but this is explicitly true: When I feel afraid, I can know God didn't send that emotion to fill my heart and mind. (Fear is different from caution. If you're running from a bear, trust that God gave you the ability and intelligence to move fast.) So if God didn't give fear to me, then I can be sure it's actually from the evil one, sent to paralyze and keep me from greatness. I make it my personal policy to not take anything from Satan, and fear is no exception. But how can we do this business of putting fear in the backseat and moving forward in courage?

Let me tell you a little secret that my son Tyler and I have for battling this monster called fear. My two children are very different in many ways, and one of their differences is their sense of reality versus fantasy. Tuck has a pretty black-and-white approach to life, and he can tell what is real and what is not. Movies and books are easy for him to digest because he can tell implicitly what is authentic and what is manufactured, what is made for thrill seeking and what couldn't ever actually happen. Tyler has no such filter. In Tyler's mind, anything and everything is a possibility. This makes him wonderfully imaginative, a brilliant problem solver, and a creative artist with ideas I can't even fathom. But such an imagination makes it difficult to read a book with vivid characters that will visit him in his sleep or to venture downstairs alone when every shadow is a dangerously looming threat. All of this has given Tyler a tendency toward timidity. Instead of seeing what could go well and right, he sees first the imminent threat.

So we started writing *Tyler's Brave Book*. In Tyler's room, he has a notebook where we record brave things Tyler does. When he went to sleep with just one night-light on, we wrote it down. When he went downstairs without an adult to the dark kitchen to fill up his water bottle before bedtime, we wrote it down. When he rode the chairlift to the top of Cheyenne Mountain Zoo, we wrote it down. When he went to the dentist, we wrote it down. When he memorized a monologue and auditioned for a show with our community theatre, we wrote it down. When he learned to ride his bicycle, guess what? We wrote it down.

Kids have to do brave things all the time. As adults, we can forget about this forced courage because one of the privileges of adulthood is deciding what you will and won't do. We can get pretty comfortable with working jobs we hate, sticking with patterns that are destructive, and living in a cozy little comfort zone because it feels too scary to do something new. We have the freedom to stop taking risks. But kids are at the mercy of the transitions of childhood. Every school year is a different teacher, new friends, even a new building. Mealtimes can call for courage as we adults place before them foods they haven't ever seen, haven't asked for, and are now forced into domestic negotiations over. We forget how brave they have to be, and it's often far braver than we're called to be.

The beauty of *Tyler's Brave Book* has become twofold. He has a growing record of his own faithfulness to himself, of when he chose courage over fear, and he has proof that he survived what he thought would take him down. But there's a second benefit, and I didn't foresee this one: He's motivated to do brave things so he can write it in his *Brave Book*. When he has a nine-year-old's challenge or a fourth-grade deadline looming, I have that golden ticket to remind him, "Just think, when you finish, you can add another page to your *Brave Book*." Something about that reward is all he ever needs to tackle the task at hand. My boy is pretty inspiring, I have to tell you.

Here's the truth about refusing fear: You can't wait until you feel safe. In fact, if it feels a little bit scary, then you're probably on the right path. The truth is that everything worth having is a little bit risky. Whether it's a relationship, a professional step, a creative endeavor, or a new adventure, there's something on the line. That's what makes it scary, and that's what makes it worth it. If you run from everything that feels scary, if you live in fear and refuse to give your heart to anything or anyone who might break it, then you'll face a different risk: boredom.

God wants us to bring everything we have to the life he has given us, and he wants us to offer it to the people around us—the people he loves. The greatest beauty of this challenge is that he wants to prove himself faithful. When Peter stepped out of the boat to walk on water with Jesus, he experienced the exhilaration that comes only with letting God show up. I imagine Peter never forgot that joyous moment, not for the rest of his life. The beauty of this is that Jesus has the same longing for our faith in him; he wants to show us how he's going to show up, to give us the adventure and exhilaration that come only with taking a risk, feeling afraid, and letting him catch us.

When I'm feeling afraid, I have taught myself to say two things to God. First, I say, "Thank you" for the thing I fear losing. After all, there's a reason I'm afraid of losing that something: It's a gift to me in the first place. Second,

I straight-up ask him to "please show up." I invite Jesus into this, to show me where he is, to be the voice that's louder than the one I don't want to hear. And then I wait and watch for him to show off.

## Stepping Forward

Make a list of dreams, ideas, and goals that you haven't put into practice because fear held you back. Next, write a timeline for when you'll try each scary thing, and write the name of a person who will hold you accountable to take that step of courage. Decide on the first step, big or small, for one of those goals. And then take it.

Start your own Brave Book. This is how you put fear in the backseat and do the next thing. When you're brave this time, it's easier to be brave next time. (And I'm a firm believer that it's always fun to write things down.)

# CHAPTER 17

# When You Feel Overlooked

## The Confident Girl Can Hope

*Hope is important, because it can make the present moment less difficult to bear. If we believe that tomorrow will be better, we can bear a hardship today.*

THICH NHAT HANH, *PEACE IS EVERY STEP*

**I HAVE A REALLY HARD** time with stories of miraculous healing. It's not because I don't believe it happened to that person, it's not that I don't believe it's possible, and it's not because I don't believe God can—and does—heal when he wants to. It's just that it hasn't happened in my life. When God gives to other people in a way he hasn't given to you, it's easy to feel left out, and it's hard to want to hear how good he has been to other people. When miracles are happening around me, sometimes the sovereignty card is a hard one to hold. It's hard to keep your confidence when you feel overlooked.

Has this ever happened to you? Perhaps you're in this

place right now, where miracles are happening all around you while you've been asking God for one. Maybe someone you love is ill with cancer, paralysis, or dementia. Maybe you or someone you love is dealing with depression, bipolar disorder, a different mental disability, or thoughts of suicide, and you're asking God to heal their mind and lift that oppression from them and from you. Maybe you live with the sorrow of infidelity or infertility, or maybe you're recovering from a miscarriage or the unspeakable heartbreak of losing a child. Maybe you're reeling with unwanted singleness. Perhaps you know how pervasive loneliness can be, especially inside a difficult marriage. Maybe you're aching over a financial crisis, an embarrassing failure, an ongoing conflict in your family, a loss of reputation, or a prodigal child you wish would come home. Maybe you wish your parents would get back together or stop fighting. Maybe you wish that your depression would go away, or that you could stop cutting yourself or start eating. Maybe you wish you could see the beauty in yourself, or maybe you wish you could disappear altogether. Maybe you have a miracle that you begged God for, and he said no. Maybe you haven't reconciled that severe brokenness, and you're still pretty angry and hurt. My goodness, I get that.

Some people claim that strong faith is defined first by throwing our energies into begging God for a miracle that will take away our suffering, and then by believing without doubting that he will do it. But faith is not measured by our ability to manipulate God to get what we want. It is measured by our willingness to submit to what he wants.

❧

Two things are unequivocally true of me: I'm a writer, and I love people. So one of my favorite things is to look closely at the characters in a story to find out about the people behind the words. That's true with any book I read or movie I watch. If I can't identify with the characters in the movie, I'll probably stop watching—and settle in with a book with more relatable characters. Since this is just how my mind works, I learn the most from the teachings of the Bible when I look at the people involved. Somehow, putting a face on these stories makes it all make sense to me. I struggled to find encouragement in a story I couldn't find myself in, and I couldn't relate to all the stories of the New Testament where it seemed like Jesus was saying yes, yes, yes. I felt like those chapters were teeming with miracles come true. In the throes of my own discouragement, I went looking for someone to whom Jesus said no, and I couldn't believe who I found: John the Baptist.

First of all, he's Jesus' cousin. When Mary told her cousin Elizabeth that she was pregnant with the Son of God, the Bible tells us that the baby in Elizabeth's womb "leaped."[1] Even before John was born, his heart belonged to the ministry of Jesus. When he was thirty years old, he began his preaching ministry near the River Jordan, and John is basically considered the precursor—the one who paved the way—for Jesus Christ. He even baptized Jesus, marking the beginning of Jesus' own ministry. When Jesus moved on to preach in Galilee, John stayed and kept preaching. He grew in power, effectiveness, and popularity—three ingredients that terrified King Herod. Whenever King Herod felt insecure or intimidated, it didn't end well for anybody.

As it turned out, King Herod was living in an incestuous marriage with his brother's wife, and John called him out on it. In a grand gesture of retaliation, Herod had him arrested and put in prison. Just like that, John was arrested and imprisoned for teaching the Word of God, for upholding what was right and true, for calling people to repent, and for making the boldest move: calling the king to repent. John was fearless. He knew everybody needs a Savior, even kings, and he spread the word. His fearlessness landed him in prison.

Here's where I began to identify with John: His thoughts got away from him, and they began to spin questions he couldn't answer about his own faith. Even though he knew Jesus so well, even though he had baptized Jesus and recognized him as Lord and proclaimed him as Messiah, things in his head started to get a little foggy as he sat inside that prison cell. He began to wonder whether anything he had ever known was remotely true at all.

While John was in prison, Jesus was in the most prolific season of his time on earth. He was doing miracles left and right while his own cousin was locked up. When Matthew told this story, he said, "John the Baptist, who was in prison, heard about all the things the Messiah was doing. So he sent his disciples to ask Jesus, 'Are you the Messiah we've been expecting, or should we keep looking for someone else?'"[2]

Essentially, John sent word: "Jesus, if you are who you say

you are, then why am I in prison? I hear about these miracles happening all over town, but I am locked up. Please send your explanation and let me know if I've been wrong all this time. I'll look for the real Messiah if it isn't you." If anyone had given his entire life to the ministry of Jesus Christ, it was John the Baptist. If anyone was deserving of a handheld miracle, it was John. He did exactly what he was supposed to do—what he was *born* to do—and he ended up in prison with no promise of rescue. This whole faith he had been professing? John wasn't buying it anymore.

I've been in that place, asking God those questions. Maybe you have been too. Maybe you've asked God questions like *How dare you? How dare you ask this of me? How dare you require this of me? How dare you allow my marriage to fall apart? I raise my kids to love you, and now they're on their own path? I've tithed my 10 percent and now we're in financial ruin? This is not what your Word promises. How dare you?* I don't know about you, but I found great comfort in reading that John had some questions too.

But here's where it gets so interesting to me. Jesus said to John's messengers, "Go back to John and tell him what you have heard and seen—the blind see, the lame walk, those with leprosy are cured, the deaf hear, the dead are raised to life, and the Good News is being preached to the poor. . . . God blesses those who do not fall away because of me."[3]

Other versions of that last verse say, "Blessed is the one who does not lose his faith on account of me" or "Blessed is the one who is not offended because of me." I had never understood that verse before. I always wondered, How can you fall away *because of Jesus?* How can anyone lose their faith *because of Jesus?* But it's beginning to make sense to me.

I think Jesus was saying,

*John, I've got a few gigs going here.*
*Yes, I am who I say I am,*
*and blessed are you if you are not offended,*
*if you do not fall away,*
*if you do not lose your faith,*
*if you can still believe that I am good,*
*if you can still obey.*

*There is blessing in this if you can still believe that*
    *I am for you.*
*Blessed are you when your life doesn't go as planned,*
*when I don't meet your expectations,*
*when I seem silent and unaware.*
*Blessed are you if you can still find hope, even if the*
    *miracle isn't yours.*
*Blessed are you if you can still hold on to your hope*
    *and your confidence in me,*
*even when I say no.*

I needed to write those words again and again, to see them on the page and begin to believe that there was a gift for me in the wake of Robb's death, that there was a blessing hidden in the truth that God chose not to heal my husband, that he let my children and me wander through a desert of loneliness and questioning and lost darkness. A long time and a lot of journal pages passed before I realized the gift in it all: intimacy with God. He gave me the gift of his faithfulness, the implicit knowledge that he was with me even when I lost what I thought I needed most.

By the way, John the Baptist never got his miracle. He was held in prison until some lovely little miss did a dance for King Herod's dinner party. We don't know much about this dance, but it's safe to believe it was an erotic, seductive dance to please the king and his guests. Sure enough, the king liked the dance, and in a grand response to impress his dinner guests, he offered her anything in the world. Her wish was his command.

She consulted her mother, who—it turns out—was the other half of King Herod's incestuous affair, the whole reason John was imprisoned. "What should I ask for, Mom? He says I can have anything at all." And her mother, who wasn't quite over John's rebuke against her, told her daughter to ask for John the Baptist's head on a platter. The king immediately sent an executioner with orders to bring him John's head, and the guy went, beheaded John in prison, and returned to the party with John's head on a platter. Literally.

That was the end of his ministry. Just like that—because of a girl's erotic dance, a woman's spiteful wish, and one gory dinner party—John was done. The next thing we read is that John's disciples heard what had happened, and they laid him in a tomb. John never, ever got his miracle. By our standards, according to the story that is recorded, he never got the miracle we would say he deserved.

Until he died. Because actually, that's where the miracle really happened: King Herod had his head on a platter, and he died. But we know that death is only a transition to eternal life. In a different story, when Jesus brings Jairus's daughter back to life, he calls her to wake up—because when Jesus is your Lord, death is only falling asleep. John *fell asleep* in prison, and he awoke in the presence of the Lord. His eternal life began, and he would never die.

My first husband *fell asleep* on my bedroom floor; I watched him die. And he awoke in the presence of the Lord. And then—*then*—he would never die. If he had been restored that night, two days before Christmas, on the floor of our bedroom, even if the paramedics had been surprised to find life sounds, even if he had come back down the stairs as a living, breathing miracle, that miracle would only have been temporary. He still would have died someday, however many years from now. And my boys and I would have grieved him then, because death always steals from somebody. None of us gets out of here alive.

And all of this—this finding hope and believing in the midst of hard things—is where faith comes into play. Hebrews 11 is the Hall of Faith, the profiles of the most profoundly faithful people in written biblical history. Paragraph after paragraph tells the story of people—real people—who acted on what they believed, not what they could see.

By faith Abel . . .

By faith Enoch . . .

By faith Noah . . .

By faith Abraham . . .

By faith Isaac . . .

By faith Jacob . . .

By faith Joseph . . .

By faith Moses . . .

By faith Rahab . . .

By faith Gideon . . .

By faith Barak . . .

By faith Samson . . .

By faith Jephthah . . .

By faith David . . .

By faith Samuel . . .

By faith the prophets . . .

By faith we . . .

By faith, by faith, by faith.

And this famous chapter is tied up with this bow at the end: "Not one of these people, even though their lives of faith were exemplary, got their hands on what was promised."[4] They all lived, and then they died, all with no tangible proof of promises kept. And *these* are the superheroes in the Hall of Faith. They are written and recorded among the greatest who said, "God, I believe you are in this, you are good, you are who you say you are, and you are for me, even though I can't understand what you're doing."

The truth is, there's no formula we can count on for when Jesus says yes and when he says no. That's the catch with sovereignty: He gets to decide yes, no, if, when, and how. We can't figure out what he'll decide, and we can't base our own confidence on his favor. We can, however, base our confidence on his faithfulness.

Miracles are temporary, but the word of Jesus, his teachings—they bring eternal life. Real life. Your faith in him and your belief that he is real, even when the miracle isn't yours, even when he doesn't say yes to you—this is what brings eternal life. If our hope is centered in this life, in what we will have while we are here, then we will forever be disappointed. But if we hope for what we do not have, if we believe God is for us, then we can wait patiently for what he has promised. Our ability to endure hardship is almost limitless—if we have the confidence to live in hope.

## Stepping Forward

Where are you struggling with God in your life? In what circumstances do you need to hear God say to you—even in the midst of your deepest longing, your deepest grief, your deepest desires unmet—"Do not be afraid; trust me"? It might begin with you simply confessing that you don't trust him. I encourage you today to start the discipline of being honest with God. Write it down, draw it, or sing it. Just promise to be honest.

My journals bind the pages of my life. I have been deeply and brutally honest with God about my anger, doubts, and loneliness. I have written down breaths of honesty I could not bear to say out loud. Saying to God, "Lord, I don't trust you, but I want to" is the beginning of hope when the miracle isn't yours. This is the root of confidence even when God doesn't say yes. Ask him to show you where he is as he says no. He'll show you: He's with you.

If you have children, give your sons and daughters the privilege of being honest with you about what they are thinking and feeling. They should be required to always speak respectfully, but they should not need to stuff down the emotions they feel intensely. Help them learn to get those questions out and examine them, to learn at an early age what each emotion feels like.

If all of this is too much, if you don't know where to begin, I recommend the search for a wise counselor, one who will let you say what you feel and be who you are, one who will gently but firmly walk with you through that black forest of emotions. These conversations can be the beginning of freedom.

# CHAPTER 18

# *Pass Your Brave Along*

## The Confident Girl Instills Confidence in Others

*Invest in the human soul. Who knows, it might be a diamond in the rough.*
MARY McLEOD BETHUNE

IN RETROSPECT—and I can only say this now as an adult—
I am actually thankful that my parents didn't pull me out
of Mrs. Wretched's class. As it turns out, some really good
and beautiful things came out of that fourth-grade year, but
I didn't know about them until twenty years later.

I had decided when I was in second grade that I wanted
to be a teacher, so while other children were merely there to
learn (how very *elementary* of them), I was studying how the
teacher was actually teaching—how she held the book for us
to see the pictures when she read aloud, how she rewarded
us with candy from her jar for following along during read-
aloud, and what shoes she wore so children could hear her
coming down the hall. (To this day, when shoe shopping,
I still have to test the sound of the shoes on the floor in the

store before I can buy them. This is because I am obsessive about some things and maybe, just occasionally, ridiculous.)

When I finally got the keys to my very first classroom of third graders, I implemented my strategic, intentional plan for how this would go. I greeted the children at the door every morning with a hug or a high five, the affection of their choice. I hung a poster on the wall that said, "Today became great when YOU got here." I taught them to be part of a community, to take care of one another and contribute to the space we shared together. We were creative in our classroom, laughing and learning in equal measure. Along the way, we met the third-grade benchmarks prescribed by the state of Colorado, despite my recurring nightmare that I arrived at school one morning to find out that it was now April and we hadn't opened our math books yet. I had an entire roster of kids ready for fourth grade by the end of our nine months together.

On a particular spring day, my students had just filled their Cup of Beans, the rewards system wherein I filled a red Solo cup with dried lima beans to reward cooperation, listening, and sunshiny days. Every time they filled the Cup of Beans, we had a classroom vote for how we might celebrate—the option to chew (sugar free!) gum for a day, wear silly socks to school, watch a movie for the last hour on Friday, have pizza or root beer floats—you get the idea. This time, they had decided to have a pajama day to finish the week.

The next morning, after I greeted the children and we

began our day, I took attendance and realized we were missing Will. A missing student without an excused absence raises red flags and alarms in a teacher's mind.

Will was hard to miss in our classroom, with his Harry Potter haircut, his loud presence, and his fierce spirit. Will and I had engaged in some serious power struggles between the two of us, and we had come to understand each other's leadership boundaries. When you fight hard with a student because you're ultimately on the same team—Team Them—they burrow deeply into your heart. Will was a classic example. I loved that tender heart behind his prickly determination, and my classroom felt incomplete without him. "Have you guys seen Will today?"

"Yeah, he was on the playground when we lined up outside this morning," they casually told me as they practiced their cursive handwriting in friendly letters to one another.

With my students busily at work, I slipped out to the playground, and I found Will sitting on the ground underneath a picnic table. He was curled into a ball, and the poor guy was wearing his jammies. Pajama day was Friday; today was only Thursday. He had worn them on the wrong day. My mind flooded with déjà vu. I had been there, done that. The scene was all too familiar to my heart. Suddenly, I was Betsy Ross on the wrong day again.

I didn't make Will come out from his hiding spot. Instead, I sat down at the picnic table, and I began to tell a story to the boy curled up underneath. "Hey, Will? Let me tell you something. . . . Once upon a time, there was a little girl in a blue dress."

As the story unfolded, Will did too. He unfurled from his tight ball of embarrassment, and he shyly joined me on the picnic bench. His courage had withered, but it began to return a little at a time as I told him about Mrs. Wretched, about my mistake, and how I never wore that dress again, not even on the right day. Will knew this: His teacher understood.

When he was finally ready, we walked inside together, straight to the office, where he called his mom to bring him clothes to wear. And Will made it through that day.

The next day, Will wore his jammies along with everybody else, including me, and nobody ever had to know. Well, not until I wrote this story in this book, but Will's okay with it. He's in college now, studying to become a teacher. (Be still my heart.)

Mrs. Wretched left her mark on me. While other teachers taught me how to do the job well, she showed me how *not* to do it. While other people taught me how to love graciously and give smiles away like they're free, she showed me what not to do. In spite of the way she crushed my spirit, I learned how to shine my light in the darkness and how to set my own confidence free. Some really good and beautiful things came out of that year, and I've learned that this may be sort of how it always goes with the worst things ever.

Mrs. Wretched stole my confidence before I even knew what that meant, and I spent a whole lot of years tracking it down and getting it back. But here's the thing about confidence: It is a gift that grows in the giving. I gave it to Will, I give it to my children, and because of God's kindness to let me write books, I get to give it to you right here, on these pages. And now it's your turn.

Having confidence means you can reclaim your story and decide what to do with it. That person who stole your confidence doesn't get to keep it. God holds every confidence, now and always, and it's free for the taking—and free for the sharing. Your vulnerability and setbacks are the very things that make you strong and brave. They are what allow you to say, "Somebody did that to me, but that wasn't the end of my story. Here's how I'm living differently. You can do it too." Someday, someone else will say, "Wait, she did *that*? Then I can do *this*."

Be brave, sweet girl. And pass your brave along. That's what confident women do.

## Stepping Forward

Is there a painful chapter, however quickly it happened or however devastating it might have been to your heart, that needs to be rewritten? You can't change history, but you can change its interpretation—and your future. Think it through; write it down. If you were a child when your confidence was stolen, view the incident through the eyes of an adult. See that situation for what it really was, and decide to believe the truth about yourself.

Keep your eyes open for the person in your life whose confidence is waning. Look for ways to pour into that individual, to tell your story and to hear theirs. Confidence grows in the giving. It is always worth your investment.

# CHAPTER 19

# Go and Be

*The Confident Girl Is Ready*

*Do the thing, and you shall have the power.*
RALPH WALDO EMERSON, "COMPENSATION"

**WE'RE ALMOST DONE, GIRLS.** The bulk of the pages are behind us, and all that's left is the journey. It's almost time to let you go, to set us all free into the world of confidence. So just before we wrap this thing up, I have a quick list of CliffsNotes for you. Because I like lists, I'm a big fan of CliffsNotes, and a go-to page of guidelines feels like a powerful finish for us confident girls.

## Guidelines to Live By, for the Confident Girl

- **YOU ARE MADE IN THE IMAGE OF GOD,** and you belong to him. There is room for you at his table and in this story that he is writing about you and with you and for you. If you do not know him as your Lord and the source of your confidence, then invite him right now to give you his eternal life. As you put your trust and faith in him alone, he stands ready and waiting to give you more confidence and assurance than you can ask for or imagine.

- **NOBODY GETS TO STEAL YOUR CONFIDENCE** for keeps. If someone has stolen your confidence from you, then go out and find it. Make confidence yours again, because it has been yours all along.

- **YOU ARE BEAUTIFULLY** and wonderfully made. This is true today and always. So don't wait too long to enjoy your beauty and appreciate the body you've been given. Also, when you find a good pair of jeans, buy two pairs.

- **YOU'RE A SMART GIRL** with a strong, amazing mind. Walk with this truth unapologetically.

- **BE CAREFUL** about who gets to speak into your life, and be mindful of the sound-bites you play on repeat. Don't put the critics in charge. If you wouldn't invite them to your dinner party, then they don't get a voice in the sacred space of your heart.

- **KNOW HOW TO BE ALONE.** *Alone* doesn't mean *lonely*, and you can be a most excellent companion to your very excellent self.

- **YOU CAN TAKE CHARGE OF YOUR LIFE** by choosing to not let it take charge of you. If you don't know where to begin, I recommend the search for a wise counselor or therapist. And if the first one you hire isn't a good fit, then move on to the next one. A good therapist can be the key to unlock your healing.

- **YOU HAVE THE RIGHT TO FEEL** how you feel. Feelings are neither right nor wrong; they simply are. It's what you do with them that makes or breaks who you become. When your heart has been broken, feel how you feel for as long as it takes. Let yourself feel; let yourself heal.

• **YOU MUST BELIEVE** that your story isn't over. As long as you are here, taking breath, then there is more for you—more to learn, more to teach, and more gifts to receive. Open your hands and receive the gifts of your story.

• **EVERYONE LOVES** to be seen and known. When they feel like you have seen them and you know them, then they love you. When people love you, then you feel more confident. It's a beautiful cycle and a revolving door. Shine your light into the world with your smile and your kindness, and watch the world bring confidence right back to you.

• **BOUNDARIES ARE A GIRL'S BEST FRIEND.** Know yourself and what you need, and then set a boundary around what you will—and won't—do.

• **LIFE IS ABOUT BLENDING,** not about balance. You'll never be able to give all the priorities of your life equal time because that isn't how life works. With so many plates spinning, you're bound to drop one from time to time. Just don't let that plate be the one you drop tomorrow. Success is in never dropping the same plate twice in a row.

• **DON'T BE SO SURE** that your next moment is more important than this one. Be present in this moment and this season, because your life is happening today. Your life is never not now.

• **CHOOSE TO NOT OVERREACT** to what scares you. Create a plan for what frightens you, and when it threatens you with worry in the dark of the night, go to sleep knowing you have a plan in place.

- **YOU NEED YOUR PEOPLE,** and they need to know you need them. Make sure they know you count on them, that you live your best life because they're in this with you.

- **CONFIDENCE IS BORN OF COURAGE,** so choose to refuse fear. It will be present, but you do not have to let it rule your decisions or your actions. Put fear in the backseat and move forward into great confidence.

- **GOD HOLDS EVERY CONFIDENCE,** now and forever. It is free for the taking—and for the sharing. So pass your brave along to someone who needs a dose of his or her own.

- **YOU WERE MADE FOR ALL THE THINGS,** and you've got this. Once more, and all together now: You can do this.

# A Joyful Commissioning

## The Confident Girl Can Do This

*I believe in being strong when everything seems to be going wrong.*
*I believe that happy girls are the prettiest girls.*
*I believe that tomorrow is another day*
*and I believe in miracles.*

AUDREY HEPBURN

**HERE. COME BACK TO THIS** table with the scones and the daisies, this place where it all started. Come sit with me one more time. Listen here, lovely one, and look me right in the eye. Are you ready? Lean in close. These words are important.

You can do this. You are smart, you are kind, you are beautiful, and even if you've never thought so before right now, you are confident. And you can do this.

As I write this last letter to you, I'm sitting at a table at Starbucks, because of course I am. And I am surprised by the tears in my eyes, these tears born of love for you, dear girl. I am praying for you this moment, praying over everything

I want for you, for us, for our daughters and our mothers, and our sisters at the dinner table and around the world who walk this earth in confidence. I pray that you will be drawn into a sisterhood of confidence, a circle of friendship that is so rich, so deep, so beautiful, and so different from you. I pray that you will bring laughter and prayer and joy and casseroles to one another when you need them most. I pray that you will have your feelings hurt, your boundaries crossed (but not too far), that you would forgive the ones who hurt you and seek forgiveness quickly from the ones you have hurt.

I ask God to give you homes that are clean enough to be healthy but dirty enough to be happy, that there will be dirty dishes in your sink, fingerprints on your windows, and stretch marks on your heart, for this will only mean you have lived with hospitality, friendship, and heartbreaking grace. I hope you'll sing in the car and dance in the kitchen. I pray that you will have friends on speed dial whom you can call in the middle of the night, and that you will be the friend who shows up when someone needs you. May you soothe babies to their comfort, hold the sick to their wellness, and walk the dying to their finish line. I hope you'll be the voice of wisdom and the song of joyful silliness, that you will know that your world needs both. May your soul long for Scripture, and may your truth be God's truth.

I pray that the God of hope will fill you with peace you can't even understand. May you stand by your convictions when you're right and experience the strength that comes with realizing and admitting when you're wrong. May you keep important secrets, give away your money, have rich conversations, and be unafraid of silence. As women, we are half of the church, and God continues to work in us and through us. We are his image bearers: gifted, empowered, intelligent, brave, responsible, and anointed. Let's embrace every confidence he has given us.

I call you to joy in everything you do—in your breakfast making, sheet changing, money making, laundry folding, team leading, note writing, toothbrushing, memory making, schedule keeping, dream building, and night watching—that you will bring life by showing up. You can do big work, small tasks, and hard things. Silence any voice that says, "Not enough." We are women, the dream keepers of our families and the world, lifting each other up and carrying the ones we love right through the trenches. May we be fearless, may we love hard, and may we nourish one another with good food and extravagant friendship.

Let's hold hands and run hard into the glorious mess of it all. This is your story, your life, your moment. Your mission field is the ground beneath your feet, and your ministry is now to the people in your world. Keep your eyes open for God's presence and have the stillness to hear him when he prompts you. He is at work. We never *have* to serve him; we only ever *get* to.

And so, on this day with the scones and the daisies, I commission you. I've said all I need to say, and now I can send you into the world, where they want you to hate yourself because they think it makes them love themselves more. But that's just not how it works, so tell them you're not playing their game anymore. The truth is that when you love yourself, everybody wins. And I've always been a big fan of love and winning.

In the mighty and powerful name of Jesus, I commission you for the work of the gospel, to live in your world as a confident servant-ambassador of Jesus Christ. Your work from now on is to bring healing, to serve and love the people around you, and to make things right in your world as much and as far as it depends on you. Remember that Gideon thought God had chosen the wrong person for the job. But God stopped the tape and called Gideon to see himself as God saw him: as a *mighty warrior*. We know that God doesn't play favorites, that he doesn't love any single one of us more than the other; and so we can know that God has put that very same strength in you. It's time today to agree with God about who he says you are.

So turn around, face your life, and jump in with all the strength you have and all the confidence you were born with. You have everything you need to begin, and we the sisterhood are here, cheering you on.

Girlfriend, you can do this.

# Great Books
# for the Confident Girl

Henry Cloud and John Townsend. *Boundaries: When to Say Yes, How to Say No to Take Control of Your Life* (Grand Rapids, MI: Zondervan, 1992).

Brené Brown. *Daring Greatly: How the Courage to Be Vulnerable Transforms the Way We Live, Love, Parent, and Lead* (New York: Avery, 2012).

Beth Moore. *So Long, Insecurity: You've Been a Bad Friend to Us* (Carol Stream, IL: Tyndale, 2010).

Rebekah Lyons. *You Are Free: Be Who You Already Are* (Grand Rapids, MI: Zondervan, 2017).

Debbie Lindell. *She Believes: Embracing the Life You Were Created to Live* (Grand Rapids, MI: Revell, 2016).

Mary Anne Radmacher. *Courage Doesn't Always Roar* (San Francisco: Conari, 2009).

Gretchen Rubin. *The Happiness Project: Or, Why I Spent a Year Trying to Sing in the Morning, Clean My Closets, Fight Right, Read Aristotle, and Generally Have More Fun* (New York: HarperCollins, 2009).

Elizabeth Gilbert. *Big Magic: Creative Living beyond Fear* (New York: Riverhead, 2015).

**ALSO BY TRICIA LOTT WILLIFORD:**
*And Life Comes Back: A Wife's Story of Love, Loss, and Hope Reclaimed* (Colorado Springs: Waterbrook, 2014).

*Let's Pretend We're Normal: Adventures in Rediscovering How to Be a Family* (Colorado Springs: Waterbrook, 2015).

# *Notes*

## INTRODUCTION: YOU CAN DO THIS
1. See Psalm 57:7, GNT.

## CHAPTER 2: WEAR YOUR NAMETAG
1. Proverbs 14:10.
2. Luke 18:1-8.
3. Luke 15:8-10.
4. Matthew 13:33, GW.
5. Matthew 9:20-22.
6. Luke 7:13.
7. Luke 10:38-42.
8. Isaiah 43:1.
9. Psalm 139:7.
10. Psalm 139:17, NLT.
11. Joshua 1:9.
12. Exodus 14:14.
13. Jeremiah 29:11.
14. Psalm 119:68.
15. 2 Corinthians 3:17.
16. Psalm 62:6-8.

## CHAPTER 5: PLAN YOUR DINNER PARTY
1. Mary Ann Shaffer and Annie Barrows, *The Guernsey Literary and Potato Peel Pie Society* (New York: Dial Press, 2009), 10.
2. Glennon Doyle Melton, "Three Rules for Surviving a Creative Life," Momastery (blog), January 20, 2016, http://momastery.com/blog/2016/01/20/three-rules-for-a-creative-life/. Emphasis in original.

3. Brené Brown, *Daring Greatly: How the Courage to Be Vulnerable Transforms the Way We Live, Love, Parent, and Lead* (New York: Avery, 2012), 56.

4. Oprah Winfrey, interview with Rob Bell, *The RobCast,* podcast audio, October 11, 2015, http://www.robbell.podbean.com.

## CHAPTER 6: THE ART OF DINING ALONE

1. Lulu Miller and Hanna Rosin, "The Secret Emotional Life of Clothes," *Invisibilia*, podcast audio, July 22, 2016.

## CHAPTER 10: SHARE YOUR KINDNESS

1. Shakti Gawain, *Creative Visualization: Use the Power of Your Imagination to Create What You Want in Your Life* (Novato, CA: New World Library, 2016), 29. Emphasis in original.

2. Judges 6:12-13.

3. Judges 6:14.

4. Judges 6:15.

5. Joshua 1:9.

6. Psalm 139:14.

7. Psalm 34:10.

8. John 10:10.

9. 2 Timothy 1:7.

10. Psalm 29:11.

11. Philippians 1:6.

12. 1 Corinthians 6:20.

13. Psalm 57:7.

## CHAPTER 11: CARRY A SHARPIE IN YOUR POCKET

1. Matthew 5:37.

## CHAPTER 12: NEVER DROP THE SAME PLATE TWICE IN A ROW

1. Bishop T. D. Jakes, Global Leadership Summit, Willow Creek Community Church, South Barrington, Illinois, August 11–12, 2016.

## CHAPTER 13: BE WHERE YOU ARE

1. Gretchen Rubin, *The Happiness Project: Or, Why I Spent a Year Trying to Sing in the Morning, Clean My Closets, Fight Right, Read Aristotle, and Generally Have More Fun* (New York: HarperCollins, 2009), 300.

## CHAPTER 15: THE UNDERBELLY OF CONFIDENCE

1. Sarah Young, *Jesus Calling: 365 Devotionals for Kids* (Nashville: Thomas Nelson, 2010).

**CHAPTER 16: PUT FEAR IN THE BACKSEAT**

1. See *Merriam-Webster's Collegiate Dictionary*, 11th ed., s.v. "foreboding."
2. See *Merriam-Webster's Collegiate Dictionary*, 11th ed., s.v. "joy."
3. Brown, *Daring Greatly*, 121–24.
4. Elizabeth Gilbert, *Big Magic: Creative Living beyond Fear* (New York: Riverhead, 2015), 26.
5. Luke 16:10.
6. Mary Ann Radmacher, *Courage Doesn't Always Roar* (San Francisco: Conari, 2009). Emphasis added.
7. See 2 Timothy 1:7.

**CHAPTER 17: WHEN YOU FEEL OVERLOOKED**

1. Luke 1:41.
2. Matthew 11:2-3, NLT.
3. Matthew 11:4-6, NLT.
4. Hebrews 11:39, MSG.